Praise for *What Are Your Blind Spots?*

"Haudan and Berens hit on one of the most powerful obstacles to creating great organizations with highly engaged people—leadership blind spots! They illustrate how many of our current leadership beliefs are suffocating the innovative, enthusiastic contributions of the people we lead. It is time to awaken the sleeping giant of human potential in our organizations, and this book provides a blueprint to do just that."

> —*Cheryl Bachelder, former CEO, Popeyes Louisiana Kitchen, Inc. and author,* Dare to Serve: How to Drive Superior Results by Serving Others

"Jim Haudan and Rich Berens have been trusted partners in shaping leadership behaviors and driving improvements in organizational engagement. *What Are Your Blind Spots?* provides invaluable insight that will help leaders in any organization—and I love how Jim and Rich bring things to life with stories and real-life experiences."

> —*Ryan Marshall, President and CEO, PulteGroup*

"In their book, *What Are Your Blind Spots?*, Haudan and Berens uncover the key emotional levers that leaders need to act on to unlock the energy, commitment, and motivation of their people. Their advice that dialogue is the only path to authentically engage the hearts and minds of our people is spot-on, and they offer powerful, practical suggestions on ways to build great relationships with people at all levels, leading to engaged, high-performing teams."

> —*Greg Creed, CEO, Yum!*

"As a leader of over 275,000 team members, identifying and understanding my own blind spots is an ongoing, continuous process. Jim and Rich tap deep into the shaping influences each of us have as leaders and the impacts of those influences on the

power and potential of our organizations. Thank you for the challenging thinking and critical exploration of my own leadership."
  —*Richard D. Maltsbarger, former COO, Lowe's*

"Berens and Haudan provide great insight into what truly drives culture change. This book is a must-read for any leader who wants to engage the hearts and minds of their people."
  —*Phil Cordell, Senior Vice President of New Brand Development, Hilton Worldwide*

"Jim Haudan and Rich Berens have been outstanding partners to our company for many years as we have tackled critical leadership and strategic issues. They have often noted that even the most experienced leaders have unconscious 'blind spots' that develop over time. In this new book, Haudan and Berens have deftly unveiled five of the most common outdated beliefs and offer practical solutions for overcoming each. I recommend *What Are Your Blind Spots?* to anyone who is serious about engaging people and achieving high performance."
  —*M. Troy Woods, Chairman, President, and CEO, TSYS*

"Berens and Haudan explore essential building blocks for leaders, which will enable them to engage their teams and drive change."
  —*Klaus Entenmann, Chairman of the Board of Management, Daimler Financial Services AG*

What Are Your
BLIND
SPOTS?

Conquering the 5 Misconceptions
That Hold Leaders Back

JIM HAUDAN and **RICH BERENS**

New York   Chicago   San Francisco   Athens   London   Madrid
Mexico City   Milan   New Delhi   Singapore   Sydney   Toronto

3 4 5 6 7 8 9   QVS   23 22 21 20 19

ISBN   978-1-260-12923-6
MHID   1-260-12923-3

e-ISBN   978-1-260-12922-9
e-MHID   1-260-12922-5

Library of Congress Cataloging-in-Publication Data

Names: Haudan, Jim, author. | Berens, Rich, author.
Title: What are your blind spots? : conquering the 5 misconceptions that hold
    leaders back / by Jim Haudan and Rich Berens.
Description: New York : McGraw-Hill, [2018]
Identifiers: LCCN 2018018928| ISBN 9781260129236 (alk. paper) | ISBN
    1260129233
Subjects: LCSH: Leadership. | Insight.
Classification: LCC HD57.7 .H3888 2018 | DDC 658.4/092—dc23 LC record
available at https://lccn.loc.gov/2018018928

McGraw-Hill Education books are available at special quantity discounts to use as premiums and sales promotions or for use in corporate training programs. To contact a representative, please visit the Contact Us pages at www.mhprofessional.com.

Contents

Acknowledgments   vii

Introduction   xi

CHAPTER ONE
Leadership Blind Spot #1: **PURPOSE** 1

CHAPTER TWO
Leadership Blind Spot #2: **STORY** 29

CHAPTER THREE
Leadership Blind Spot #3: **ENGAGEMENT** 53

CHAPTER FOUR
Leadership Blind Spot #4: **TRUST** 77

CHAPTER FIVE
Leadership Blind Spot #5: **TRUTH** 107

CHAPTER SIX
Assessing Your Leadership Blind Spots
and Lessons Learned 135

Notes   149

Index   153

Acknowledgments

Any endeavor as significant as writing a book truly tests the network of friends and supporters you have in your life. Together, we leaned on a number of people who meaningfully contributed to making this book possible. These very special people include Veronica Hughes, Victor Zhang, Adam Hastings, Nolan McNulty, Karen Proffitt, Aleassa Schambers, Erin Kanary, Angie Hyatt, Brad Haudan, Kristen Fritz, Ryan Tapscott, Bridget Stallkamp, Lindsay Camp, Aleassa Schambers, Erik Szymanski, and Jessica Greer. We also had the wonderful pleasure to work with the well-known American editorial cartoonist Henry Payne. Henry brought wit, humor, and insight into depicting what many people feel as they experience the five leadership blind spots. The sharp thinking that goes into his illustrations is brilliant. Two special individuals made sure that our passion behind this project turned into a coherent story worth telling. Together they project managed, improved, and enhanced the quality of the book throughout the crafting and refining process. Without Anne Urfer and Dawn Martin, this book would still be a notebook containing various ideas. Thank you to every one of you for being the village that raised and graduated *What Are Your Blind Spots?*

To our editor, Cheryl Ringer, a huge thank you. Your challenges to make what we had to say clear, simple, and profound helped make our work as reader-friendly as possible. It was your advice that helped us land on an appropriate title. Your coaching on the chapters helped us create both energy and connectivity to unify our story.

From Jim

Really sustainable partnerships and partners are rare. When you find a partner who complements your weaknesses, elevates your play, role-models your aspirations, and is someone you are constantly learning from, you are very lucky. Rich Berens is that partner. He is a confident and humble servant leader who is constantly focused on helping make others more confident, capable, and successful. I am very grateful to be on a shared journey with him to find breakthroughs in the ways leaders can engage and unleash the power of their people. In reality, Rich is the example of what can happen to invigorate people when a leader infuses the passion of purpose, builds a story of adventure for the future, engages people with curiosity and excitement to co-think the business, trusts that everyone is more creative and capable than they believe, and relentlessly pursues understanding the truth behind what's working and what's not. He creates an environment where people contribute the very best they have to offer every day. He is a friend, thought partner, business partner, and one of the best leaders I know. Writing this book together is a very special privilege that I tremendously cherish.

My wife, Michelle, has taught me that compassion and excellence are a powerful mix that truly leads to finding "better ways" to impact the lives of people around us. We were just kids when we first met, but after 40-plus years together, I am deeply grateful for her love and still intensely driven to make her proud. My adult children and their spouses—Brad and Jenny, Brooke and Pete, and Blake and Mary—never cease to amaze me with how much I can learn from them. Your strong self-esteem, reverence for family, spirit of service, and quest for lifelong learning are awe-inspiring. Thank you to our five grandchildren, Gabrielle, Nick, Ali, Cam, and Sloane, who constantly cause us to rediscover the awe and wonder of being a grandparent.

From Rich

This book is the result of endless hours of co-thinking, co-creating, and co-writing with my friend, mentor, and business partner, Jim Haudan. It represents many of our experiences over the past 20 years, and the opportunity to process them together and co-author this book has been one of the highlights of my work life. Jim is a marvelous business thinker and speaker and an even better human being. There is not a person I would have rather co-written a book with.

This book would also not be possible without my great family. My wife, Anne, is my rock, and I am incredibly grateful for her smarts, compassion, and unquestioning support. My daughters, Katarina and Mia, inspire me every day, and I hope that this book is an example to them that whatever you set your mind to, you can accomplish. They are growing up to be intelligent, funny, and most importantly, kind young women, and I can't wait to see what mark they choose to leave on the world.

Introduction

It was December 12, 1799, and George Washington, at 67 years of age, was just over 30 months into his retirement from being the first president of the United States of America. Never one to sit still, he was very involved supervising activities at Mount Vernon, his estate in Virginia. His property spread over more than 500 beautiful acres along the Potomac River. He spent most of that December day outside, and an entry in his diary that evening about the weather conditions read, "About 10:00 it began to snow, soon after it hailed, and then a settled rain." The following day, he complained of a sore throat but went out again on his horse to mark trees that he wished to be cut. It was another cold day punctuated by heavy snow and hail. Despite not feeling great, he returned home in good spirits. He spent the evening with his wife, Martha, and his personal secretary, Colonel Tobias Lear, reading various newspaper articles aloud and discussing them to the degree that his hoarse voice permitted. When the colonel suggested he take medication, Washington replied, "You know I never take anything for a cold. Let it go as it came."

At 2 a.m., he awoke with severe shortness of breath. His wife wanted to go out and get help, but ever the gentleman, he did not want her to be exposed to the elements, as she had suffered from a cold not long before him. Martha asked for Colonel Lear to come into the room to help with the situation. Gravely concerned, they quickly sent for physicians, three of whom would make it to the estate the next day. Washington was a big believer in bloodletting and asked his estate overseer, George Rawlins, to start the process. Rawlins removed between 12 and 14 ounces of Washington's blood that morning before the physicians arrived.[1, 2]

Bloodletting was for centuries one of the most common practices used to treat severe headaches, fevers, and almost any other significant ailment you could think of. It worked by using a sharp piece of wood or a sharp knife to open a vein and allow blood to flow into a container. While its origins seem to come from ancient Egypt, it really took hold with the Greeks. Hippocrates, a Greek physician, built on the beliefs established by Greek philosophers that the four basic elements of existence were earth, wind, water, and fire. He claimed these elements were represented by four "humors" in humans: blood, phlegm, black bile, and yellow bile. When humans got sick, these four were out of balance, and bloodletting was a great way to rebalance them. Somehow this seemed to make a lot of sense to people, and the treatment became popular. It was used in the Roman Empire, the Indian and Arab worlds, and the Western world until the eighteenth century. And as is obvious with this story, it was a method still widely accepted and applied when Washington got his cold.[3, 4]

As the doctors arrived at Washington's bedside, they tried various ways of providing comfort to the first president and trying to improve his condition. The one thing they did consistently was bloodletting. There were four more sessions of bloodletting, removing well over 80 ounces of Washington's blood. To put that in context, they removed 40 to 50 percent of his blood in one day!

Washington grew weaker throughout the day, and by that evening, he said to his doctors, "I feel myself going. I thank you for your attentions and I pray that you take no more troubles about me. Let me go off quietly. I cannot last long." He died a little after 10 p.m.

What exactly did he suffer from? This is still debated in medical circles today. But we do know that losing half his blood that fateful day was anything but helpful. And amazingly enough, Washington himself was a big proponent and was advocating to the physicians that this needed to be done.

You may ask, How could someone who was instrumental in the creation of the Constitution, who was the first president of a system of government that has stood for over 200 years and is a model for a modern democracy, and who was, by all accounts, a brilliant man, believe in something this nutty? How could physicians be blind to the fact that most of the time they were doing way more harm than good with the method of bloodletting for centuries?

This is merely one example of a belief or approach becoming the acceptable and "best" way to do something, even though in hindsight it is obvious that it is not. Let's explore a few more examples of rather peculiar methods and beliefs that manifested themselves broadly.

WE REALLY BELIEVED THIS?

The World Is Flat

For thousands of years, it was a widespread belief that the world was flat and that if you went to the edge of it, you would fall off. Aristotle was one of the earliest to dispute this belief and provide evidence against it. He simply stated that when one travels south, the constellations appear higher above the horizon, which would not be possible unless the earth was round. But more than 1,500 years later, the belief in a flat earth was still widely accepted as true.

Cocaine Cough Drops

There are many beliefs that society has held even in the more recent past that are a bit shocking when viewed through the lens of today. Nowhere is there a more jolting example than the use of cocaine as medicine for kids' everyday ailments. In Figure I.1, you see an ad that ran in 1885 for cocaine drops for toothaches—for children.

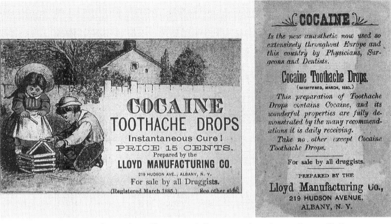

FIGURE I.1 *An advertisement for cocaine-laced medicine for kids from the 1890s*

We are not making this up. The medicine not only promised to relieve pain but also promised to provide a lift in mood! We can just see the dialogue between parents:

"Honey, Annabelle seems to be a bit cranky and not herself today."

"No worries. Just slip her one of the cocaine drops in the cupboard, and she will be off."

Smoking

Smoking is probably the most well-known example of where our beliefs have changed profoundly over the past 50 years. U.S. Surgeon General Luther Terry's 1964 Advisory Committee Report on Smoking and Health provided the catalyst for a sea change in our societal perception of smoking. Prior to that turning point, our attitude toward smoking was very different. Smoking was socially desirable, did not raise meaningful health concerns, and was as common as drinking a glass of wine with dinner is today. You could hardly find a movie star or musician who wasn't holding a cigarette or promoting a brand for that matter. Figure I.2 shows the "Rat Pack" members Dean Martin, Sammy Davis Jr., and Frank Sinatra who defined cool in their era and were rarely caught without a cigarette in their hand. In fact, as you can see in Figure I.3, smoking was so socially acceptable that many advertisements touted the health benefits of smoking and frequently used doctors as pitchmen.

FIGURE I.2   *"Rat Pack" members Dean Martin, Sammy Davis Jr., and Frank Sinatra were rarely found without a cigarette in hand.*

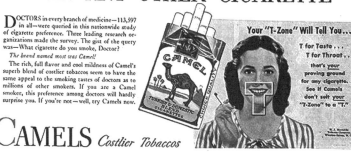

According to a recent Nationwide survey:

MORE DOCTORS SMOKE CAMELS THAN ANY OTHER CIGARETTE

DOCTORS in every branch of medicine—113,597 in all—were queried in this nationwide study of cigarette preference. Three leading research organizations made the survey. The gist of the query was—What cigarette do you smoke, Doctor?

The brand named most was Camel!

The rich, full flavor and cool mildness of Camel's superb blend of costlier tobaccos seem to have the same appeal to the smoking tastes of doctors as to millions of other smokers. If you are a Camel smoker, this preference among doctors will hardly surprise you. If you're not—well, try Camels now.

Your "T-Zone" Will Tell You...

T for Taste...
T for Throat...
that's your
proving ground
for any cigarette.
See if Camels
don't suit your
"T-Zone" to a "T."

CAMELS *Costlier Tobaccos*

FIGURE I.3 *Doctors promoting cigarettes were commonplace in the 1950s.*

Soda

In the past few years, we have become much more conscious about carbonated soft drinks and their impact on our health, especially their adverse effect on children, including the rise of childhood obesity and diabetes. Today a number of cities have implemented a special tax on sugary beverages in an attempt to curtail consumption. The link between sugar and childhood obesity is well established these days. But that was not the case at all a few decades ago. Look at Figure I.4 and see how 7-Up positioned its drink in the 1950s to be a great choice for your toddler.

FIGURE I.4 *An advertisement touting the benefits of carbonated soft drinks for babies and toddlers*

Here is the actual text in the ad in Figure I.4:

> This young man is 11 months old—and he isn't our youngest customer by any means. For 7-Up is so pure, so wholesome, you can even give it to babies and feel

good about it. Look at the back of a 7-Up bottle. Notice that all our ingredients are listed. (That isn't required of soft drinks, you know—but we're proud to do it and we think you're pleased that we do.) By the way, Mom, when it comes to toddlers—if they like to be coaxed to drink their milk, try this: Add 7-Up to the milk in equal parts, pouring the 7-Up gently into the milk. It's a wholesome combination—and it works! Make 7-Up your family drink.[5]

HOW DO EXAMPLES FROM OUR PAST RELATE TO COMPANIES TODAY?

The point is not to pick on particular companies and question their marketing campaigns. Instead the point is that beliefs and approaches that now seem absurd were not only embraced by many people; they were actually promoted and endorsed by the leading companies and experts of the time. They were legitimate societal blind spots that, in retrospect, make us shake our heads in disbelief at what we accepted as good or desirable.

Only in hindsight do these things seem silly, absurd, or at best misguided, as they were considered perfectly normal at the time they were practiced. Not until our beliefs were challenged and we had new insights and deeper levels of understanding did we challenge our ways on a broad scale.

WHAT IS A BLIND SPOT?

Traditionally the phrase "blind spot" refers to a part of the retina that is insensitive to light, which results in an actual spot in the eye where a person can't see. "Blind spot" is also a phrase used when the side mirrors of a car create a space to the left and right side of your vehicle where you can't see cars passing or driving next to you.

Just as we have visual blind spots and societal blind spots (noted earlier), we have found, in our 20+ years of working with many of the largest companies across all industries around the world, that there are leadership blind spots. We define leadership blind spots as *areas where our existing beliefs and experiences preclude us from having the most enlightened view of how to lead most effectively.*

The research that linked smoking to cancer and sugar-filled, carbonated drinks to obesity wasn't always obvious. But if you take the time to reconcile data with reality, you can embark on a trajectory of profound belief challenge and change. In short, you can overcome a particular blind spot. Our point in this book is that there are a series of leadership blind spots that cloud how we lead and run organizations and the people in our organizations. These blind spots are just as absurd as concepts such as bloodletting, cocaine toothache drops for kids, healthy smoking habits, and wholesome, carbonated soft drinks mixed with milk. And like those societal blind spots, we aren't aware yet of how flawed our thinking is when it comes to our leadership. We claim that several years from now, we will look back at how we run organizations today and shake our heads at how unenlightened some of our practices and beliefs were.

CHANGE STARTS WITH OUR BELIEFS

Many of our current beliefs about how organizations should run date back to the Industrial Age! In his book *Why We Work,* Barry Schwartz explains that many of our thoughts about work, and the role of employees, have been shaped by none other than Adam Smith, the famed eighteenth-century economist, philosopher, and author of *The Wealth of Nations.* Smith's work has been instrumental in how we think about and run our businesses, and much of it has been taught in business schools as foundational knowledge since their inception. Smith wrote: "It is in the inherent interest of every man to live as much at his ease as he can; and if his emoluments are to be precisely the same whether he does or does not perform some very laborious duty, to perform it in as careless and slovenly a manner that authority will permit."

In a nutshell, the core belief established here is that people's primary, if not sole, motivation for working is . . . money. And people will do as little work as they can possibly get away with in order to get that money. While this is not the most desirable state of mind from a human perspective, it worked reasonably well in the Industrial Age where division of labor into smaller, repeatable activities was the way to be the most productive.

Today we are well past the Industrial Age; we are somewhere between an information age and an experience economy. People still care as much as ever that they get paid and that they get paid as well as they can. But we also know that people are motivated by being a part of something larger than themselves, by feeling a sense of belonging and connectivity, and by knowing that their contributions make a difference. Yet many of the beliefs from the Industrial Age about how to run companies and how to treat people have stuck with us. And while many leaders intellectually understand the difference, we time and time again see beliefs, habits, and practices that are remnants of the old way of leading. It seems that 200+ years of habits are hard to break!

It's time to help free leaders from some of their long-held and no longer relevant beliefs regarding human nature in the workplace. The leadership blind spots that we will learn about throughout the book are destructive forces that work against engaging the workforce, creating results, and effectively competing in today's world—and are remnants from an era that has long come and gone.

WHY THESE BLIND SPOTS MATTER

Our goal in this book is to shed light on the five most common leadership blind spots. The stakes are high, as the realities of today's workplace scream for an intense examination of the core beliefs from which all leaders lead and engage their people. We know that 60 to 90 percent of all strategies are not executed, 70 percent of people in organizations are not actively engaged, and annually, more than a half a trillion dollars' worth of economic value is not realized in the United States alone as a result.[6, 7]

Picture your organization or team in a tug-of-war with the competition to win more customers and grow your business. Assume your company consists of ten people you have on your side of the line to help you win, as illustrated in Figure I.5. The data tells us that while three people are pulling as hard as they can to win, five of your people are not pulling at all—they are pretty much indifferent. And two people are trying to cut the rope with a knife and set the rope on fire at the same time.

ENGAGED   **INDIFFERENT**   **ACTIVELY DISENGAGED**

FIGURE I.5   *The engagement tug-of-war*

While this isn't a pretty picture, it is an accurate representation of most workplaces today. Studies show that 50 percent of the people are indifferent, 20 percent are actively disengaged or are arsonists, and a mere 30 percent are actively engaged. What's even worse is that this picture has not changed for 30 years. That's right! According to Gallup's annual employee engagement polls, there has been no significant movement in engagement scores in the last 30 years. That data is staggering!

During this same time, we have seen dramatic changes in some of our most pressing social issues, like a reduction in cancer deaths and traffic fatalities or, as discussed earlier, a decline in smoking habits or consumption of highly sugared drinks. We have made significant progress in many areas—but not in the way people show up to live the majority of their life at work! In the words of author Lisa Earl McLeod, "Work is competitive, work is hard, and work can be exhausting. But it shouldn't be soul sucking awful." Everyone should have the right to do work that is meaningful, engaging, and productive. And every leadership team should be obsessed with making that happen. Not just because it is the right thing to do. It is also simply smart business.

So what can we do to facilitate change? The first step, and typically the hardest, is realizing and accepting the fact that this disengagement is not your people's fault. Most professionals don't wake up each day and say, "I can't wait to *not* make a difference today," "I am indifferent about what we do as a company. Just pay me," or "My goal for the next year is to be average at best!" The great majority of us don't want to think this way about the place where we spend more time than anywhere else in life—and yet way too many of us feel that way.

While all employees should own their engagement, the truth is that the tone, conditions, and environment in which those same employees could thrive or become disengaged are set by leaders. Change has to start with leaders, and it has to be about owning and creating the conditions for high engagement and high performance. Yet leaders often don't know how to create those conditions, or worse, they don't fully believe in the importance of creating those conditions.

THERE ARE LIGHT BULBS IN THERE!

As a real-life example that stuck with us, a few years ago we had the privilege of working with one of the top ceiling tile manufacturers in the country. The company was experiencing significant change driven by foreign and domestic competition. There was price pressure, a need to revisit the effectiveness and efficiency of its North American manufacturing plants, and a need to engage its workforce in that change. The company was also starting to use a new measure—EVA (economic value added)—to gauge financial success and build a companywide gain-sharing plan to do so.

Our charge was to engage every employee in the organization in the change. To do that, we needed to engage people in the changing dynamics of the marketplace to ground them in the "why" of the change. We also needed to make them comfortable with the EVA-based gain-sharing system and create a link between that and how their day-to-day activities connected to all of it.

We carefully crafted the storyline and developed learning materials to enable robust and thoughtful two-way conversations. One of our first stops for a pilot was a manufacturing plant near Macon, Georgia, where about 12 plant employees joined us for the session.

This was a group from all walks of life, largely men, ranging in age from their mid-twenties all the way up to their early sixties. They were hard workers, and while they appreciated time off their shift, none of them looked ecstatic to see a couple of consultants about to walk them through "a business literacy program." They had seen these types of workshops before and had a healthy skepticism about our true intentions and what other shoe would be likely to drop in the next two hours.

Our goal for this meeting was to get the employees at this plant engaged in thinking about the challenges of the business and identifying solutions. A member of our team started to facilitate the session while a couple of us observed the room with the plant manager, Larry. It was clear that Larry's job was being dictated by an order coming from above rather than one he fully embraced. As things got going, he kept sighing and shaking his head and was all but openly annoyed by the whole process.

At the front of the room, the conversation with the group started out slowly. Our process had the group work through a series of questions, and we were getting radio silence, likely because there was a combination of skepticism around our intent and trepidation around the content itself. While no one was saying much of anything, it was pretty clear what the people assembled were thinking:

"Are these guys here to evaluate us?"
"Will there be layoffs?"
"Why is Larry watching this whole thing?"
"This looks complicated, and I don't want to look stupid."

This went on for a couple of minutes, and we could see that Larry was getting increasingly agitated. One of us leaned over and whispered to him, "Hey, Larry, we have to give this a bit of time and let them play with the information and it will work out great. We need to just stay quiet back here and not make them nervous. It will be amazing once you see the light bulbs go on."

What follows is one of our all-time most memorable client quotes. Larry looked at us funny, leaned over, and said, "You've got to understand. My people ain't got no light bulbs, and we are in for a long afternoon."

Now we were all really nervous that Larry was not going to give us the benefit of the doubt, but conversation eventually began to pick up. Two hours later, we had the group of 12 actively engaged in the market, the gain-sharing plan, and what was and wasn't working around the company. When the session wrapped up, we went around the table and asked for feedback and reflection from each participant.

What happened next has vividly stuck with us to this day. A man who was in his late fifties went first. He said, "I have worked here for over 20 years. And for 20 years I have been told what to do." And then he got teary-eyed, with his lips trembling a bit, and he said, "This is the first time someone has asked my opinion about the business, and I just want to say how thankful I am for that."

Not only was our team blown away and moved, but we could see that Larry was as well. The comment hit him at his core, and we are pretty sure we changed Larry a bit forever that day. The rest of the debrief echoed the same sentiments. When we shook hands at the end, Larry looked us in the eye and said, "You know what? I need to do a bit better looking for the light bulbs in people." Larry realized he had a major blind spot in how he was operating his plant and engaging with his people. At his core, he didn't trust his people and expected little; therefore, he got little in return. That day had him rethinking his management belief system and showed him that he needed to operate differently.

What a powerful "aha" for him to have. Unfortunately, Larry's story is not an unusual one. We see similar stories time and again at all levels of leadership and in all industries. The world is littered with Larrys—leaders and managers who underestimate, underappreciate, and underutilize the potential of their people. And when given the chance to see differently, they are dumbfounded at the untapped interest, intelligence, and creativity of their people. When leaders are placed in a situation as Larry was, their beliefs usually surface, including "They won't get it," "They won't care," "They won't see it as their job," and "They won't be motivated to step out of their comfort zone." And all are instantly challenged by this experience.

The truly dark side of that leadership belief is not the lost productivity, but the impact on the average employee. There is a great sense of untapped value and appreciation that people have about their jobs. A large number of employees simply don't feel valued, and because of that, they show up indifferent about their jobs.

Take a second and ask yourself these questions to get a better understanding of both yourself and your people:

- When was the last time you felt really listened to?

- When was the last time you felt that anything you said made a meaningful difference?
- When was the last time the work you did felt really valued?
- When was the last time you felt that your efforts contributed to winning?
- When was the last time you could connect your actions to business results?

If the answers to these questions don't excite you, you are not alone. We have, for the most part, a systemic level of disengagement in our workforce.

One of the greatest untapped opportunities in business today is to access the dormant human capital that we often fail to capture and inspire. With only 30 percent of professionals being engaged, the vast majority of human talent is not showing up at work to innovate, create, build, change, and find better ways of doing things. As leaders, we simply can't accept that. We have to look in the mirror to get at the root causes of this challenge and uncover blind spots in order to create a better way of leading.

After 20+ years of working with over 850 global companies and having touched over 10 million people in those companies, it is our strong conviction that a set of leadership blind spots accounts for the difference between those who get it and have great, thriving, and growing workplaces and those who don't.

Just think of it: What if we did not have workplaces where 30 percent are actively in the game and 70 percent are indifferent or worse, but where those numbers were reversed? Think of the tremendous potential for innovating, collaborating, and finding new ways of serving the customer. Think of teams you have been on and meetings you have been in where the majority of people were fully immersed and engaged. How productive were you? How much faster did you move the needle? How much more fun did you have? The energy, positivity, and goodwill of a highly engaged team create an almost unstoppable force. If we are able to do that, think of the benefit we create even beyond more profitable and thriving enterprises. We create a more enlightened world with better organizations, where people are striving to be at their best rather than just trying to get through the day.

THE BLIND SPOTS IDENTIFIED

We have identified five leadership blind spots that perpetuate disengagement and indifference. They do the exact opposite of creating thriving, innovative workplaces that turn customers into advocates and fans. Let's take a quick look at each one before each chapter breaks them down further and answers the key questions leaders need to ask themselves in order to see things as their employees do.

Leadership Blind Spot #1: Purpose

Common Misconception. Purpose matters, but it doesn't drive our numbers.

The Basics. While there was a time when employees were only paid to complete a specific set of tasks, there is way more to it than that today. Many leaders are starting to embrace the concept of purpose but fail to actually run their businesses in a purpose-driven way.

The Question We Will Answer. As leaders, how can we put purpose at the center of the way we operate our business and achieve exceptional financial results because of it?

Leadership Blind Spot #2: Story

Common Misconception. We have a compelling story to tell that our people care about.

The Basics. Most organizations have a semigeneric vision statement, accompanied by what seems like too many slides to outline their strategy for what winning looks like for the organization. Leaders believe they have a compelling story to tell, but when seen through the eyes of the employee, the complete opposite is often the case.

The Question We Will Answer. What makes a strategy story compelling, and how can we craft one for our people?

Leadership Blind Spot #3: Engagement

Common Misconception. Rational and logical presentations engage the hearts and minds of people.

The Basics. In many organizations, a tremendous amount of money is spent creating strategies to win. Those strategies then get communicated using PowerPoint presentations, road shows, or town hall meetings—but things seemingly get stuck. Employees fail to connect with the strategy, leaders are frustrated about the lack of progress, and managers just try to hold the ship together.

The Question We Will Answer. How do we move from presentations to conversations and create genuine engagement in strategies in the business?

Leadership Blind Spot #4: Trust

Common Misconception. People will not do the right thing unless you tell them what to do and hold them accountable to do it.

The Basics. Companies want and need to deliver great service to differentiate themselves, and the common belief is that the best way to deliver this is to create tight processes, scripts, and routines that minimize variability—to hold people and their behaviors to a strict policy and uniform standards. But that approach will never create consistent yet unique, differentiated, and personalized experiences that lead the market.

The Question We Will Answer. How can we trust and scale the unique human judgment, discretion, and care of our people, while at the same time having firm standards that we all share?

Leadership Blind Spot #5: Truth

Common Misconception. My people feel safe telling me what they really think and feel.

The Basics. In many leadership teams, what people really think often gets discussed in the hallways and bathrooms and by the watercooler rather than in meeting rooms. People don't feel safe telling the truth because they don't think it is smart or safe to do so. Many leaders believe that to be effective and successful, they need to be smarter than the next guy, fight for their area of the business, and not show vulnerability. This mentality creates lack of trust, collaboration, and common ownership for a greater goal—and ultimately greatly slows down execution speed.

The Question We Will Answer. What can we do as leaders to make it safe for our people to tell the truth and act on those truths to make the business better?

The next five chapters will explore these five leadership blind spots in detail through stories and experiences that we have been a part of over the last 20 years. We are pretty sure we were not always the smartest guys in the room, but we were able to take a lot of notes and see firsthand how these leadership blind spots play out, and more importantly, what some of the very best are doing differently to create thriving workplaces and successful companies.

CHAPTER ONE

Leadership Blind Spot #1: **PURPOSE**

Common Misconception
Purpose matters, but it doesn't drive our numbers.

The Basics
While there was a time when employees were only paid to complete a specific set of tasks, there is way more to it than that today. Many leaders are starting to embrace the concept of purpose but fail to actually run their businesses in a purpose-driven way.

The Question We Will Answer
As leaders, how can we put purpose at the center of the way we operate our business and achieve exceptional financial results because of it?

INCREASE REVENUE OR SAVE BABIES?

We had the opportunity to host a senior executive team of a global company focused on quality and safety standards in our water, food, and consumer products. This company conducted an engagement survey and found that its employees were disillusioned about the company. The company leaders then created an internal task force to dive deeper into what was behind the discontent. They brought their executive team and several of the task force members to our facilities to reveal their findings and discuss the implications openly. The task force members opened the day with a very telling slide, shown in Figure 1.1.

To be crystal clear, this is a company whose job is literally to save babies by making sure the water we drink, food we consume, and toys we play with are indeed safe. Yet people in the company had a difficult time connecting the dots between how the company was run and how the strategies, metrics, and activities they were undertaking linked to the larger purpose of the organization.

This is not uncommon. Connections aren't always clear, and this results in frustration within the workforce. But on the flip side, we have also seen many instances where it was the conviction in the importance of purpose that was lacking.

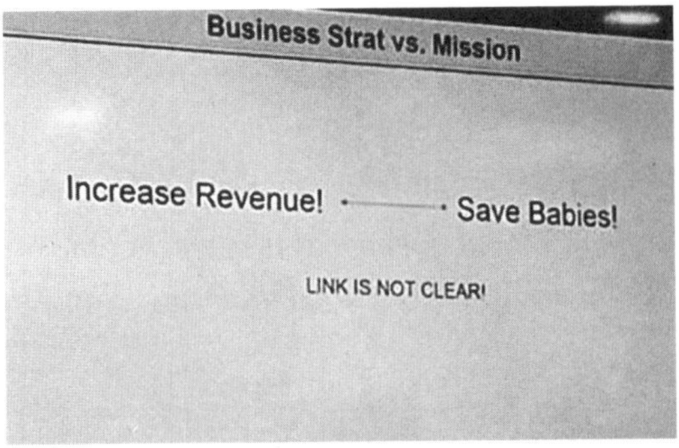

FIGURE 1.1 *A client slide demonstrating the struggle on how to link purpose to the company's core business metric*

A few years ago, we worked with a large industrial conglomerate. It was a successful organization, and the CEO, who was in the latter stages of his career, had ambitions to more thoroughly shape his legacy in the organization by creating a greater focus on the company's purpose. Creating a lasting purpose would be something he passed along to the next generation of leaders by setting a path for a successful future.

The process of establishing a legacy included the creation of a purpose council that was made up of a broad set of representatives from the organization. The council had numerous global conference calls where people had the opportunity to share their perspectives and ideas on what the purpose of the organization should be. The members of the council looked at the origins of the company and where it was at the time, and then they did some real soul-searching on what they wanted the company to stand for as it moved into the future. The process included numerous broader listening sessions and, of course, a consultant with expertise on how to become more purpose driven. While a bit tedious, the effort was sincere, and progress was being made.

A few months in, the business results were under pressure, and quarterly numbers came in quite a bit lower than expected.

We were sitting with the CEO over dinner when the subject of purpose came up. He told us, "The purpose work is important, but we have hit some headwinds. It's time to really focus on the operations of the business and get the numbers moving again. We can then go back to our purpose work once we have things under control."

On the surface, that sounds very rational, but it was essentially an admission that the company lacked the belief that focusing on purpose is an important performance driver for the business. Unfortunately, we see this all the time. Purpose becomes something that a company only focuses on when things are going well or we have extra time on the agenda.

....

This gets right at the heart of the first misconception we have encountered many times with leaders: Purpose matters, but it doesn't drive our numbers. This misconception is all too common across many executive teams. These teams acknowledge that purpose is important, but they don't really believe it's essential to business performance.

In study after study, the vast majority of respondents, often as high as 90 percent, said that their company understood the importance of purpose, but less than half thought that their company was run in a purpose-driven way.

In our experience, leaders are reluctant to replace the existing belief that purpose and profits are largely separate endeavors. The former is seen as "soft" and something to tell stories about to build corporate pride and connectivity, while the latter is a nonnegotiable and something that should be managed weekly. As a result, the concept that purpose is an enabler of superior results and should be a central guide of your business strategy is not a common belief for most of today's leaders. That belief is compounded by a corporate ecosystem that makes it exceedingly difficult to build a high-performing, purpose-driven organization for the long term. In the words of one of the CEOs we interviewed for the book, "All the stuff you guys are talking about is bullshit in the eyes of many at the top, and they just don't care." And for those who do, the deck is stacked against them (even though that shouldn't be the case).

The challenge starts at the business school level where many are still taught that shareholder value is the true north of organizational purpose, a concept that Jack Welch, the former CEO of GE, has called "the dumbest idea in the world." This concept focuses on the shareholder as the primary stakeholder and making money at any cost, as long as you stay within the appropriate legal and regulatory boundaries.

To compound the challenge, the investor community is dominated by "short-termism." The length of time that investors hold stocks has moved from eight years in the 1960s to less than five days today![1]

The focus is all about the next quarter and whatever levers you can move to beat the estimate. And when it comes to those leaders who actually want to create a purpose-driven organization, it is an uphill battle against conventional wisdom and the accepted norms, behaviors, and actions of how things work today.

So what do we do to change this mindset? We believe the answer lies in every leader asking this fundamental question that gets at the core of how an enterprise is run:

> Am I creating an organization that focuses on bringing its purpose to life every day, or am I creating an organization that is focused on hitting the numbers every day?

In order to get to the honest answer, try answering these three questions to determine whether or not your organization is purpose driven. The actions suggested underneath each question provide you with a simple way to get an honest snapshot of the role that purpose truly plays in how your business is run.

- **Question:** Are your meetings primarily about the numbers, or do you have active conversations on the purpose and how to activate it?
  Action: At the next three strategically focused meetings you attend or lead, gauge how much your purpose is shaping the agenda and the conversations of team members.

- **Question:** What does success for the business look like?
  Action: Ask 10 people in your organization this question and see what they mention first. Is it financial goals or the impact we are looking to have through what we do?

- **Question:** What does the company's purpose mean to you? How personally meaningful is it to you?

  Action: Go into a bit more detail on purpose and ask five people what the company's purpose means to them personally and how they believe it impacts the customers and communities it serves.

Of course, being purpose driven and having financial success are not mutually exclusive. It's just the opposite. But the conversations you have and how you run your organization are very different based on what your primary driver is.

THE RISE OF PURPOSE

Research has shown a more than fivefold increase in publications writing about purpose since 1994, with most of that increase happening in the past five years. And interestingly enough, the content of the articles has shifted from whether purpose matters to how to authentically bring it to life and have it be meaningful for a business.[2]

Why is purpose so much more prevalent in business today? After all, did our moms and dads and grandmas and grandpas not care about these things when they were working? Did we not care a mere few years ago when people were not talking about this as much?

Show Me the Money

There are numerous factors at the core of why purpose is moving to the forefront. One key reason is that there is now a growing amount of literature and studies backing up its impact. A pacesetter for this was Jim Collins and Jerry Porras's 1994 book, *Built to Last*. This book found that between 1926 and 1990, a group of so-called visionary companies was guided by a purpose beyond making money, and each business returned six times more to shareholders than explicitly profit-driven companies.

One of the more recent pacesetters of this thinking is the Conscious Capitalism forum. In a study looking at stock returns of purpose-driven companies and captured in the book *Firms of Endearment*, the authors found that the "Firms of Endearment" outperformed the S&P over a 15-year period by a ratio of 10 to 1.[3]

There is a lot of data coming in that shows purpose-driven companies are outperforming the market. Executives tend to like data, and it is telling them loud and clear that this is something they need to pay attention to.

If It Ain't Broke, It Might Actually Already Be Broke

Just as great success stories have fueled purpose, so have stories highlighting the failure of organizations that did not have a clear purpose at their core. Let's look at Blockbuster, which was a well-oiled machine, renting movies to customers through thousands of retail stores around the United States.

Blockbuster was in an industry that was facing enormous change, as technology was allowing competitors to reach customers directly first through mail delivery and then streaming. This shift all but eliminated the need for retail stores. As the marketplace changes gained momentum, Blockbuster was not able to adapt quickly enough and went from the biggest player in the industry to bankrupt within only a few years.

There are obviously numerous factors that contributed to Blockbuster's failure, and being the incumbent when industries change can be very difficult. But a key reason for its inability to adapt was that Blockbuster was not purpose centered at its core in a way that it could positively reshape its business. It was not focused on finding the best way to bring content and entertainment to customers. Instead it was focused on serving customers and maximizing profit of an established retail store model that had more than 9,000 stores at its peak. When the market changed, the company did not have a purpose strongly guiding it to adjust to the new rules of the market.

As one poignant example, there were many internal battles that took place within Blockbuster on whether it should waive its late fees. Customers hated the fees, and the competition was making movies available for much longer via mail order without charging. But the company and its stores were so addicted to the profit that late fees generated that Blockbuster could not get itself to stop charging them until it was way too late. You could ask how a group of smart people could not see the bigger picture. One key lesson is that Blockbuster had an operating model and financial targets as its true north guiding its strategic filter, rather than an externally focused purpose doing that.[4, 5]

There are many Blockbuster-type examples that line the graveyard of fallen titans. The reasons for failure are manifold. But one of the core reasons is that companies fall victims to their existing operating models and financial expectations and lack the ability to reframe where and how to compete. Organizations with a strong purpose at their core are more likely to be able to change when they truly need to. They will view their current operating model and customer offerings as merely a means to achieve their larger purpose and should therefore be able to change direction more easily when market forces require a more radical shift. Blockbuster viewed itself as being in the primary business of renting movies via its stores. If the company had a bigger purpose, it would have realized it was in the business of providing entertainment to customers whenever and wherever they wanted—and it might still be around.

Soul-Searching After the Financial Crisis

The financial crisis and severe economic recession of 2008–2009 created soul-searching for many companies and employees about why they do what they do and what success looks like. Maybe one of the few benefits of that calamity was that it got many of us to look collectively in the mirror and ask what we like and do not like about the companies we run or the companies we work for. Blatant, untethered greed and the devastating consequences demonstrated by some key players within the financial services industry had an impact on many of us. Don't get us wrong—making money is essential for any organization, and profitable enterprises should be celebrated and embraced. But it became more and more obvious which companies had money as the sole or primary driver of success.

A Decline in Trust

According to the Pew Research Institute, Americans' trust in our government has declined from 73 percent in 1958 to 19 percent by 2015.[6]

While trust in corporations and their leadership has not declined quite that precipitously, it has dropped quite a bit as well. The lack of trust has, unfortunately, become a bit of an epidemic with seemingly no end in sight. Many of us yearn to have institutions and leaders we can trust in. When trust declines, transaction costs go up. When you are unsure about a product you may buy, a doctor you may use, or a leader you work for, what do you do? You ask around to see what you can learn from peers you do trust; you do your own research; you determine all your options and become skeptical about everything you hear and hedge your commitment. That is very different from when you have full trust. You are likely to skip most of those things and just purchase from those you have established trust with.

The decline in trust has made us, as consumers, more skeptical while also being much more loyal to the organizations, people, or products that we authentically trust at the same time. With that being said, the purpose of a company winds up being a major factor when it comes to customer decisions—and organizations are becoming more and more aware of this.

While the quest for organizations with shareholder value as the sole true north has created efficient, agile, and focused organizations, it has also created companies without a soul. And it turns out a great many of us don't like buying from or working for that type of organization. As a matter of fact, many of us actively dislike working for those organizations, and if we have a choice, more and more of us choose not to. In his book *Why We Work*, author Barry Schwartz explains that "work is more of a frustration than one of fulfillment for nearly 90 percent of the world's workers. Ninety percent of adults spend half their waking lives doing things that they would rather not be doing at places they would rather not be!"

In many ways, the financial crisis has accelerated or triggered a long-term shift in how we determine what businesses we buy from, what company we work for, and what type of experience we want when we go to work. And this fact is only accelerating with millennials entering the workforce. This generation expects organizations to be purpose driven, and if you are not, you're out. Period.

Our society is at the beginning of a long-term and likely permanent shift where purpose is a core driver of our decisions on where we work and what brands we are loyal to. We will support organizations that are purpose driven and will continually move away from those that are not. Figure 1.2 shows the mindset of employees and customers alike when it comes to who they want to work for and buy products from. Leadership teams are feeling that, and it is why purpose is gaining traction and is part of conversations not just in boardrooms, but also among employees and consumers now more than ever.

But therein lies the challenge. Becoming purpose driven and developing a purpose statement seems to be a convenient answer, but it's not that easy. Adopting a purpose and having a purpose statement doesn't in any way guarantee that you are actually pur-

FIGURE 1.2 *People are drawn to purpose-driven companies more than ever.*

pose driven. What we see in many organizations is the notion that we can't be caught without a purpose, but then it's time to move on and run the business without it playing an integral role in guiding us. We can guarantee you that your people will see through that, and the effort will result in eye rolling and cynicism rather than the desired long-term competitive advantage.

WHAT CREATES A POWERFUL PURPOSE?

One of the foremost thinkers on purpose in recent history is Simon Sinek, who has published several books and gives an excellent TED Talk titled "How Great Leaders Inspire Action." According to Sinek, purpose is not about what you do, but it is about why you do what you do. It's the big-picture answer to the question, "What is your reason for being as an organization?" Most companies have spent time working on "the what" and "the how" but have not really gained deep clarity on "the why." And absent that, you are more strategically vulnerable to not adjust to today's environment of rapid change. You are also vulnerable to the chance that your people will not have an authentic and meaningful connection to your company, leaving them feeling more like a cog in a wheel.

If you are not sure how to authentically make purpose the driver of your company, try this. Look at any successful person or company in history that you admire and really listen to the conversations about that success. Watch people tell their company story or observe how people passionately discuss what they do. In almost every case, the idea that they are a part of something bigger than themselves will surface.

When Tim Cook, the CEO of Apple, was asked to only commit to those activities that were profitable, he responded by saying, "When we work on making our devices accessible by the blind, I don't consider the bloody ROI." That goes for many areas Apple pursues. According to him, the company does "a lot of things for reasons besides profit motive. We want to leave the world better than we found it."[7]

Apple is one of the most profitable companies on the planet and has been for some time. Cook's point is not that Apple doesn't care about profits. But profits are merely the outcome of being a company that is focused on creating unique value for its customers and doing things the right way. Cook knows that is important to him, to the people working at Apple, and to most people buying Apple products. It's not only the right thing to do; it is actually the smart thing to do.

While a meaningful purpose is important, it's also crucial to understand that this can raise difficult questions that teams need to be ready to wrestle with. CVS is the perfect example of such a situation. In September 2014, CVS stopped selling tobacco products because such products went against its purpose of helping people on their path to better health. The company understood it would take a significant short-term revenue hit, but the purpose of the company was the main driver.

After a few months of not selling cigarettes, CVS conducted a study of the impact this change had in states where its pharmacy share was prominent. The results were astounding. The company found that tobacco sales in those states across *all* retailers decreased by 1 percent in an eight-month period. That is a reduction of five packs per smoker and an overall reduction of 95 million packs of cigarettes in those states! That is living your purpose.

While CVS lost significant tobacco sales, the company also gained a lot of respect from many customers and employees because it showed it was serious about what CVS stands for. The jury is out, but we would venture to guess that over a 10-year time frame, this will prove to be a very profitable strategic decision embraced both by CVS employees who feel that there is an authentic commitment to purpose and by customers who show a greater degree of loyalty and trust toward the company.[8]

Purpose ultimately requires great conviction and courage from leaders. Their focus must be on something larger than themselves and creating or fostering that in their organizations.

CREATE AND TEST YOUR PURPOSE

Being a purpose-driven organization is hard work. It requires an organization to have an honest and authentic purpose that intellectually and emotionally resonates with people. Organizations where purpose really takes hold often take it one step further and invest in their people gaining a greater clarity of their own personal purpose at work and how that connects to the larger ambition of the organization. Both ideas together can unleash game-changing performance, and we will explore them next.

Not surprisingly, one of the first companies to capture the power of purpose in business before it was on anyone's radar screen was Disney. Van Arsdale France worked for Disney in the 1950s, founded the University of Disneyland, and was a key contributor in bringing Walt Disney's dream of Disneyland to life. He was passionate about pitching his larger idea about connecting every employee to that larger dream and "get everyone we hire to share in an intangible dream, and not just work for a paycheck."

In his pitch to Walt Disney and the rest of the executive team, he said, "Look, the purpose of Disneyland is to create happiness for others. . . . You may park cars, clean up the place, sweep the place, work graveyard, and everything else, but whatever you do is contributing to creating happiness for others."[9]

While a statement like this can be a powerful beginning, it is the spirit within and throughout the organization that is most important. Take Apple again. Its true north is to think differently. Apple believes that products should be beautiful and that interactions should be intuitive and inspirational. And we all know that is exactly what Apple products do. Before Apple, this was difficult to say about any product in the technology space. So what makes an effective organizational purpose statement?

Create Your Organizational Purpose Statement

We have seen dozens of different purpose statements of varying quality. The meaningful and most effective ones tend to share four qualities. They are outlined in Figure 1.3. In reviewing the four guidelines in this figure, you will get a better understanding of how to create an effective and meaningful organizational purpose statement.

FIGURE 1.3 *Purpose guidelines*

We will use our organization, Root Inc., and the thought process we went through as an example that might be helpful before you get started thinking about your organization:

What is your organization's desired impact on people or the world at large?

> *We are dissatisfied with the fact that it is OK that the majority of people in the workplace are disengaged and we want to unleash the human capability that is silent every day.*

What would be reflected in a purpose that is unique to you?

> *The engagement of people in a way that connects their hearts and minds in the business story.*

How would your organizational purpose provide strategic inspiration?

We need to build services and capability to help leaders be better leaders, managers be better managers, and individuals be better contributors. We also need to be sure that in a rapidly changing world of technological innovation, we do that in a way that is relevant and meaningful to today's workforce.

What is there about your organizational purpose that would speak to the head and the heart?

It is really important for us that we invigorate and inspire people to not just want to change, but to lead the change. That often starts at work, but when we invigorate them the right way, it impacts all aspects of their life.

Now go ahead and answer these questions with your own organization in mind. Once you have done this, review your notes and take a few minutes to create a draft purpose statement for your own organization. If you already have an organizational purpose, there is an activity at the end of the chapter to test its strength and effectiveness.

What is your organization's desired impact on people or the world at large?

_____

_____

_____

What would be reflected in a purpose that is unique to you?

_____

_____

_____

How would your organizational purpose provide strategic inspiration?

_____

_____

_____

What is there about your organizational purpose that would speak to the head and the heart?

_____

_____

_____

Now look at your notes for all four questions and take a few minutes to create a draft purpose statement for your organization. Following is our company's purpose statement, which you can use as inspiration for getting started, and below that is a place for you to create your own statement.

Root's Purpose Statement

*Invigorating the power of human beings
to make a difference*

Your Company's Purpose Statement

_____

_____

_____

_____

Once you have a statement you feel excited about, run your ideas past a few other people and see if they have similar thoughts about the four guidelines and your purpose statement draft.

Organizational Purpose in Action

In the book *Leading with Noble Purpose,* author Lisa Earle McLeod asks a powerful question: "What if your work mattered so much to you that—on your deathbed—you found yourself wishing for one more day at the office?" She suggests that while we may have all heard that no people on their deathbed wish that they'd spent more time at the office, it is intriguing to consider, what if we did? What if we authentically felt that way? A way where the same quality of experiences and relationships that we expected and nurture in our personal lives we found and experienced in our professional lives. Boy, would that shatter the current apathy and indifference in the workplace! Better yet, what if we lived a life where a day with those we love and a day at the office with those with whom we share a common purpose had a similar sense of importance, meaning, and joy?

Arguably, the best comment McLeod leaves us with is this: "We have allowed the money story to replace the meaning story."

She argues that we have made some faulty assumptions about work, and those assumptions support a belief structure that meaningless or purposeless work is OK.

The most humbling and special experience both of us had when it comes to the impact of being a purpose-driven organization was when we were together at a business meeting in Chicago and received a voice mail. It was from Arden Brion, a managing director of our healthcare practice. He had been near Philadelphia earlier in the day for a presentation with a prospective client, and during the meeting he had felt shortness of breath and a tearing in his chest and was losing his strength. He was quickly rushed to the hospital, where he was diagnosed with an acute ascending aortic dissection, Type 1. In laypeople's terms, it means a tear occurred in the aorta, causing blood to flow between the layers of the aorta. This often compounds itself, and the artery essentially starts leaking blood, frequently leading to rapid death. It is what the actor John Ritter died of unexpectedly in 2003.

The doctors had diagnosed Arden that afternoon and told him that the odds were greater than 95 percent that he would not survive. He had about 90 minutes until they put him under and operated, and the attending ER physician suggested he make final phone calls to his family.

After Arden called his family, his next call was to us, and it was a message we will never forget. He thanked us for the wonderful times we had together and the privilege it had been to work for the company. He mentioned several people within the company he wanted us to pass his thanks on to. He was simply grateful and wanted to wish us a happy goodbye while he still could. He said that working for Root was one of the great privileges of his life, and it allowed him to make a difference.

We were tearing up, concerned, and stunned that with perhaps less than 90 minutes to live, Arden had called us—guys he was working with. It speaks of tremendous grace on his part, and the message was one of the most reaffirming things either one of us has ever experienced as a leader.

Most importantly, Arden beat the odds, and we had the privilege to visit him in the ICU a couple of days later. We now celebrate his "new birthday" each year, and Arden just celebrated his new-life fourth birthday!

While that is thankfully an unusual circumstance, the situation does raise the question of how many people in the organization would be excited to spend additional time in their job helping you deliver on your purpose.

The Importance of Conviction

In order to activate purpose at your organization, your leaders must have conviction in that purpose while also being clear on their personal purpose at work. People generally have a desire to bring their best selves to work, but if you or they are not sure what that best self is, it's hard to consistently bring it or know when and where to apply it. Great organizations don't just have an organizational purpose, but they bring out personal purpose in individual people as well.

When we talk about personal purpose, we don't mean an all-encompassing answer to what makes you happy in life. That's a bonus. We are referring to understanding what makes you happy and most effective at work. As a leader who wants to be truly purpose driven and have teams that are as well, you must ask yourself the following questions:

- Do I know what drives, motivates, and inspires the people working on my team?
- Do I know the core strengths and passions of my team?
- Do I know what each person's personal best is and understand how to activate it?

- Do I know the personal purpose of the members of my team?
- Do I help individuals bring their purpose to life?
- Do I know how to connect people's personal purposes to the larger purpose of my organization?

Once you can answer yes and elaborate on each of your answers, you will be ready for a game-changing performance.

Simon Sinek wrote in his book *Start with Why:*

> Studies show that over 80 percent of Americans do not have their dream job. If more knew how to build organizations that inspire, we could live in a world in which that statistic was the reverse—a world in which over 80 percent of people loved their jobs. People who love going to work are more productive and more creative. They go home happier and have happier families. They treat their colleagues and clients and customers better. Inspired employees make for stronger companies and stronger economies.[10]

If you want to create an organization in which 80 percent of your people are excited to come to work and are vested in the success of the business, your people need to know and feel that you are fully vested in their success. They need to see how they connect to the purpose of the organization and how their contributions make a difference.

Test Your Organizational Purpose

Now that we have the purpose statement that we worked on earlier, let's work on testing the effectiveness of this purpose. While you can do this work on your own, it is best to have a team of three to five people work through these questions together.

Decide on the strength of each guideline, and circle the strength on each of the four dimensions shown in Figure 1.4; then draw a line connecting each number you circled to create some form of a square. If you are working as a group, it can be of great value to do this activity individually first and then compare how each of you rated your organizational purpose statement.

Insert your current organization purpose statement:

_____

_____

_____

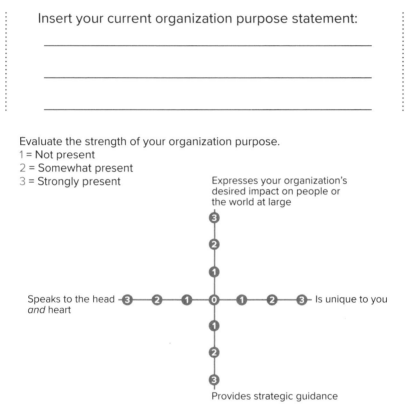

Evaluate the strength of your organization purpose.
1 = Not present
2 = Somewhat present
3 = Strongly present

Expresses your organization's desired impact on people or the world at large

Speaks to the head *and* heart

Is unique to you

Provides strategic guidance

FIGURE 1.4 *Test the power of your organizational purpose.*

Next see where you might be able to improve your statement. For guidelines that were ranked below a 3, write down ideas for how you might be able to strengthen your purpose statement:

_____

_____

_____

Write a new purpose statement integrating your ideas:

_____

_____

_____

Purpose Gut Check

Let's apply one other filter to help gain clarity on the tangible impact your organizational purpose statement should have on your key stakeholders. How will your organizational purpose statement help you drive greater impact for . . .

Your customers?

_____

_____

_____

Your people?

_____

_____

_____

Your other stakeholders (shareholders, community, etc.)?

_____

_____

_____

Once you have an organizational purpose statement that you feel both you and your team are connected to, allow this to be an enabler to your business. Really think about how you can embed it into the day-to-day activities of your business.

- How does your purpose shape or influence your strategic planning?
- How are you integrating your purpose in your communication and engagement with others?
- Where and how is it getting integrated into critical meetings as a discussion point to drive action?
- Where and how is it getting integrated into the mindsets, habits, and skills of your organization?
- What are your mechanisms for celebrating when you see your purpose being activated in a powerful way?

Link Personal Purpose to Company Purpose

Now that we've created, tested, and refined our organizational purpose, we need to establish our personal purpose as well. But before we get there, let's take a look at a real-life story that shows exactly why it's so important to have both.

Steve S. had played football at the high school level and had a legitimate aspiration to land a scholarship in college—that is, until Steve suffered a knee injury that ended his ability to compete. All that Steve had envisioned of how his next few years would play out changed overnight. Playing the game he loved in front of thousands of fans was no longer possible. While this, unfortunately, could have set Steve back, he refocused, attended the U.S. Naval Academy, and years later is the senior executive of a large restaurant chain.

The experiences of suffering through that injury and finding a new course for his life stayed with him and shaped his perspective and thinking—so much so, in fact, that Steve's personal purpose at work now is to create a safe place where people are comfortable taking risks and can reach their full potential.

Steve's newfound focus was a game changer for the company. His organization had significant growth ambitions and a desire to open over 500 franchises in a very short time frame, and Steve was at the head of this companywide change. But the culture of the organization was such that taking risks was avoided because it seemed like the safer and smart thing to do. Enter Steve. His personal purpose was perfectly suited to creating an environment at scale where it felt safer to take a risk and pursue the ambitions of the company. Steve helped his team lead the way in opening up hundreds of new restaurants around the world and being a major growth driver for the company.

Create Your Personal Purpose Statement

Steve's story is the perfect example of how important it is to have both an organizational and personal purpose. We have found that organizations that create the time and space for people to create their own personal purpose are more effective in truly embedding organizational purpose into their companies. Creating a personal purpose statement will establish a meaningful connection to your work and help you to become the best possible version of yourself at the office.

Before creating your own personal purpose, let's use Steve's story as an example that might help you think about yours.

Steve's Personal Purpose Statement Worksheet

What are your work and life experiences that shaped you as a person?

The physical injury in athletics forced me to change course and embrace the risks of a new adventure.

What are the unique skills and talents you can offer the world?

Get comfortable with the unexpected and turn it into a growth opportunity.

Imagine you are reflecting at the end of your career. How would you want to be remembered as a leader? What is your impact and legacy?

To be remembered as someone who helped people get comfortable with the discomfort of risk taking.

Considering the reflections above, write your personal purpose statement:

Create a safe place where people are comfortable taking risks to reach their full potential.

How does your personal purpose statement best serve your organization?

I was able to inspire a team to lead the international expansion of the organization by opening over 500 franchises in rapid pace around the world.

Now take 10 to 15 minutes to work through these same questions to establish your personal purpose statement.

Personal Purpose Statement Worksheet

1. What are your work and life experiences that shaped you as a person?

_____

_____

_____

2. What are the unique skills and talents you can offer the world?

_____

_____

_____

3. Imagine you are reflecting at the end of your career. How would you want to be remembered as a leader? What is your impact and legacy?

_____

_____

_____

4. Considering the reflections above, write your personal purpose statement.

_____

_____

_____

5. How does your personal purpose statement best serve your organization?

_____

_____

_____

CONNECTING THE DOTS

Most leaders have dealt with personal and organizational purposes superficially without fully recognizing either and therefore are not activating purpose authentically and effectively within their organizations. This first leadership blind spot all but eliminates the true impact and effectiveness that truly purpose-driven organizations possess and why they outperform.

While we may have overcome the first blind spot, this is only the beginning. Chapter 2 explores why stories, or lack thereof, can be responsible for wasting millions and may be hurting your company more than you know.

CHAPTER TWO

Leadership Blind Spot #2: STORY

Common Misconception

We have a compelling story to tell that our people care about.

The Basics

*Most organizations have a semigeneric vision statement,
accompanied by what seems like too many slides to outline
their strategy for what winning looks like for the organization.
Leaders believe they have a compelling story to tell, but when seen
through the eyes of the employee, the complete opposite is often the case.*

The Question We Will Answer

*What makes a strategy story compelling,
and how can we craft one for our people?*

Psychologist Elizabeth Newton conducted an experiment while working on her doctorate at Stanford in 1990. She gave one set of people, whom she called "tappers," a list of commonly known songs from which to choose. Their task was to rap their knuckles on a tabletop to the rhythm of the chosen tune as they thought about it in their heads. A second group of people, called "listeners," were asked to name the songs.

Before the experiment began, she asked the tappers how many songs they thought the listeners would be able to identify based on their taps, and their answer was about half. The results were quite the opposite. Listeners only got 3 out of 120 songs, or 2.5 percent, correct. The tappers were astounded. Each song was so clear in their minds. They wondered how it was possible that the listeners couldn't "hear" it in their taps.[1]

Experts or leaders sometimes experience a similar reaction when they set out to share their ideas in the business world. So many leaders struggle to engage people in the strategy of their organization because their story makes sense in their own head, but to everyone else it seems confusing, boring, and largely irrelevant. And most of the stories that leaders have created lack cohesiveness, clarity, drama, and a sense of what is possible. Most of the time, leaders are excited to share the strategy and often think they are doing a heck of a job, while for everyone else it feels more like a foreign film with subtitles. We are talking about one of those where it's hard to read all the language on the screen and keep up with the plot and you stay with it because you love your spouse who has a liking for foreign films.

Just about every company that Root Inc. works with struggles with its story—even the great ones. While these standout organizations provide great services and make great products, they fall flat when it comes to crafting an effective story to engage their people on the strategy and the future of their business. And as Figure 2.1 shows, what's worse is that most leaders think that they are effective

FIGURE 2.1   *Most strategy stories are anything but compelling.*

and that they have a hit on their hands, while the opposite tends to be true in the eyes of their employees.

That brings us to our second leadership blind spot, story, and the outdated belief that goes along with it: We have a compelling story to tell that our people care about.

WHY DOES TELLING A COMPELLING STRATEGY STORY MATTER?

We have worked with many executive teams, and it is not unusual to see eye rolls when we talk about strategy storytelling. It is often perceived as a soft topic, despite its importance. Connecting your strategy and decisions in a meaningful way to hundreds or thousands of employees is crucial to bringing your strategy to life. As author Stephen Denning writes, "Analysis might excite the mind, but it hardly offers a route to the heart. And that is where we must go if we are to motivate people not only to take action but to do so with energy and enthusiasm."[2]

The truth is that to reach the heart, you have to create a sense of adventure and a sense of belonging, while also outlining a meaningful journey where people can see how their contributions make a difference. Jerome Bruner, a famous Harvard professor of psychology, made the point that our Western scientific worldview is largely concerned with facts and truths. While of course facts are important, we fail to use storytelling to give those facts and truth meaning. You need both aspects to be effective, but most organizations only focus on one. The way organizations typically create and share their story simply does not create meaning, and it leads to strategy stories that people don't care about and can't connect with.[3]

There are four components that contribute to creating a compelling story. We will explore them in detail throughout this chapter. They are:

1.   Having a vision statement that is a great headline to your story
2.   The quality of the strategy story that supports your vision
3.   Your ability to share your story effectively as a leader
4.   Achieving shared meaning of your story by your leaders

HAVING A VISION STATEMENT THAT IS A GREAT HEADLINE TO YOUR STORY

As purpose in the previous chapter gave us the *why* we exist as an organization, a compelling strategy story provides us with the deeper meaningful narrative of *what* winning looks like.

Most companies do this with a vision statement, a supporting strategy deck, and key metrics. And that is where things start to break down.

Let's dig deeper into vision statements and where leaders start getting themselves into trouble. For the sake of a common defini-

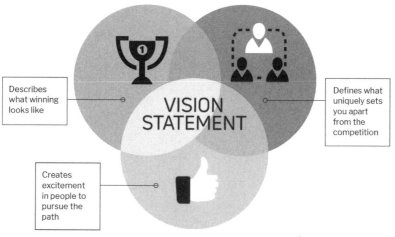

FIGURE 2.2 *Characteristics in a vision statement*

tion as shown in Figure 2.2, let's call it the statement that describes to your organization what winning looks like, defines what uniquely sets you apart from the competition, and creates excitement for people to pursue the path.

Compelling vision statements need to represent a powerful headline to your strategy story, but most of the time they don't. Unfortunately, in many organizations the vision statement is a result of too many leaders wordsmithing something that is shockingly uncompelling, generic, and unhelpful.

We were working with the members of the leadership team of a multibillion dollar firm in North America that wanted to develop a new vision. They were somewhat risk averse and asked us to look at how their peers approached the issue to get a starting reference point. We did some of that research and came back to present the vision statements without sharing the names of the companies.

We reviewed these statements through a few lenses, shown in Table 2.1. As you read through the samples on the left side of the table, fill in your answers to each question at the top of the chart. We filled in the first one to get you started.

TABLE 2.1

Vision Statement	1. What industry is this company in?	2. Are you clear on what winning looks like for the company? (Yes or No)	3. Are you clear on what differentiates this company? (Yes or No)	4. Are you compelled to get out of bed in the morning to pursue these ambitions? (Yes or No)
We will become the world's most valued company to customers, colleagues, investors, business partners, and the communities where we work and live.	Not clear	No	No	No
Our vision is to be the world's premier [industry] company. Simply put, we want to be the best—the best employer, the best supplier, the best business partner, the best investment, and the best neighbor.				
Our vision is to lead the way to a healthier world. By carrying out this vision at every level of our organization, we will be recognized by our employees, customers, and shareholders as the best [industry] company in the world, resulting in value for all.				
We are a performance-driven culture that uses metrics to ensure continuous improvement. Through our distribution and marketing competencies, we provide creative, customized solutions for our customers. As a result, we achieve superior profit growth as the [industry] provider of choice.				

34

What feeling did you get as you read each of the four vision statements? As you tried to assess if the statement was connected to an industry, was clear about winning, was clear about differentiation, and was compelling, what did you think? Additionally, did the statement provide you with great clarity, meaning, or a sense of excitement? Probably not—and yet these are representative of many vision statements that we see. Unless you were in the room creating these vision statements, they likely have little meaning to you. None of them provide clear guidance in terms of what winning looks like and what makes each player unique, and none of them are inspiring.

As we worked with the members of the executive team from this pharma organization, they could not identify the names of companies that went with each of the statements within their industry, and it became clear to all of us in the room that there was limited value to any of these vision statements. This evaluation allowed the participants to take a step back and think differently about what their vision needed to accomplish and how it could be an effective headline for the strategy.

Now read the vision statements in Table 2.2 and apply the same filter. See if you can guess which company each statement belongs to.

While we are not endorsing these companies or their strategies, their vision statements are very well done. Each statement defines a desirable future for that company in compelling and understandable language, while also articulating the unique path each organization will take to get there.

TABLE 2.2

Vision Statement	1. What company is this?	2. Are you clear on what winning looks like for this company? (Yes or No)	3. Are you clear on what differentiates this organization? (Yes or No)	4. Are you compelled to get out of bed in the morning to pursue these ambitions? (Yes or No)
At [company] our vision is to create a better everyday life for the many people. Our business idea supports this vision by offering a wide range of well-designed, functional home furnishing products at prices so low that as many people as possible will be able to afford them.				
Our vision is to be Earth's most customer-centric company; to build a place where people can come to find and discover anything they might want to buy online.				
[Company] designs, manufactures, and launches advanced rockets and space-craft. The company was founded in 2002 to revolutionize space technology, with the ultimate goal of enabling people to live on other planets.				

Answers: Ikea, Amazon, SpaceX.

For Amazon, it is to be the most customer centric and provide customers the ability to find and discover anything. For Ikea, it is well-designed furnishings at the lowest possible prices, and for SpaceX, it is to revolutionize space technology to launch advanced rockets and spacecraft and ultimately enable living on other planets. These are powerful concepts that are compelling and give clear guidance. They also use understandable and emotive language.

One additional and very important point: As you think about the headline of your strategy story, you have to make sure that you don't lead with a number as your true north. We worked with a large technology company a few years ago to help engage its 20,000+ employees in its strategy.

When we asked what winning looked like for the company, we were repeatedly and unequivocally told that it was to more than double the revenue to $60 billion in the next five years. It was *the* rallying cry for the organization. And while there was excitement around the financial possibilities that could be created for key players, it wasn't all that meaningful for most of the employees. This "money-only" vision statement created endless conversations in the field about how much money the executives were going to make, about who had stock options and who didn't, and about how reaching that number was going to stretch the workforce beyond their limit. None of it was about creating anything exciting or compelling. It was not about redefining an industry, disrupting how things are currently done, or creating something radically new or a breakthrough for their customers. Instead, it was about a *really* big number.

Don't get us wrong. Numbers matter greatly to a business and are the ultimate tally on whether your value proposition resonates with customers. But the company failed to engage people in the answers to some important questions including: What is the adventure we are pursuing together? What are we looking to create that does not yet exist? Why should we be excited to be a part of that journey beyond a big number? The number has to be an outcome of what you create. It should never be the destination.

Continually ask yourself how you think about your business. Is your true north of what winning looks like a metric, or do you have a compelling vision that headlines the adventure ahead?

As you review your own vision statement, be sure that it:

- Clearly articulates what winning looks like
- States what makes you unique
- Creates a sense of adventure to find a better way that inspires and creates followership

If you feel you have a compelling vision statement, your next challenge is to be sure that the storyline supporting the vision is compelling and easy to understand—and creates connection points for people to their work.

THE QUALITY OF THE STRATEGY STORY THAT SUPPORTS YOUR VISION

One of the most important jobs that leaders have is to inspire people to embrace change. After all, if they can't do that, it is really hard to scale any idea, process, or new strategy. The key is to paint a picture of a compelling journey and outcome with enough detail to provide guidance for action and change. As Stephen Denning said in his article "Telling Tales" in *Harvard Business Review*:

> [It] should whet a listener's imaginative appetite about the future without providing detail that will likely turn out to be inaccurate. Listeners should be able to remold the story in their minds as the future unfolds with all its unexpected twists and turns. And clearly, the story should portray that state in a positive way. People are

more likely to overcome uncertainty about change if they are shown what to aim for rather than what to avoid.

This is where the traditional PowerPoint deck that most companies rely on gets them in serious trouble. The way we construct our stories and share our strategies is driven by numbers and bullet points and is void of emotion, narrative, and meaning. As a matter of fact, most presentations are quite good at making compelling content extraordinarily dull.

Most businesses have incredibly interesting stories, full of drama and interesting plot lines. That holds true for most industries, as just about all are going through rapid change driven by technology and a new set of nontraditional competitors, and evolving customer expectations are the norm.

Let's take the auto industry, which we have worked with for many years, as an example. This has long been a fascinating industry with several of the large players such as Toyota, GM, Ford, VW, Honda, Daimler, BMW, and several more battling for global and regional supremacy. If you are a leader in any of those organizations, you are looking at an incredibly interesting story ahead with many strategic crossroads.

How do you continue to stay ahead of your traditional competitors in established markets as well as growth markets like China? How do you think about rapidly emerging competitors like Tesla, which are offering breakthrough design and electric engine technology as well as a direct selling model to reach the consumer rather than going through a dealer network? How do you think about companies like Uber, Lyft, mytaxi, and dozens more that are redefining the need for car ownership and are leading the way toward a new mindset of transportation as a service rather than a product you need to own? How do you think of new financial technology entrants that might redefine your model of how people finance their vehicles and, in the process, may learn more about your customers than you know?

The amount of money invested in these areas is in the billions of dollars, and the pace of innovation is incredible. The various storylines for each player are fascinating and can be more captivating than most of your favorite television dramas. Yet in most companies, the stories we tell are mundane and uninteresting, leaving our people disconnected from the story and uninterested in truly taking part in the adventure that is our business.

If Steven Spielberg can take just about any story and make it interesting and something you can identify with, most leaders take a story as compelling as *E. T.*—one of his masterpieces—and make it come across like *Gigli*. (It's worth looking up if that collaborative project between Ben Affleck and Jennifer Lopez doesn't ring a bell. This is the authors' opinion, but we do believe the movie has to be partially responsible for their breakup.)

It is the leaders' responsibility to craft a storyline that creates the connections as well as the intellectual and emotional buy-in for people to want to go on your journey. It becomes the responsibility of the leader to make sure that your employees want to watch that movie that is your strategy. You have to have the mindset that it is *your* job to have them want to internalize your story, rather than their job to have to listen to it and figure out where the excitement is.

If you are wondering how to best build a story with your team, one process we use is handing out five Post-it Notes to each executive on the team. We then ask each of them to identify five different components of their future story that are most compelling to them and write them on separate Post-its. Once everyone is finished, we collect all the notes and group them by themes on a large wall. So, for example, if there are numerous Post-it Notes relating to innovation, we would put those together in one column.

Each member of the executive team then reads a column aloud while the others listen. Next, each member chooses just three notes that really stick out to the member as being critical to his or her strategy story.

Once all other notes are removed, the group members are asked to create a comprehensive and compelling story using the notes left on the wall as the reference point. From here, we create an outline of what they said and visualize it in a larger sketch format of roughly three by five feet. The goal of this sketch is to capture the essence of the story and how the key pieces within it connect to one another. We typically iterate this visual story two or three times to refine it and make sure that it is focused on the right audience, has a strong overarching message, and captures the core drama.

STORY CREATION ESSENTIALS

A few key concepts must be established when creating and delivering an effective story. Each and every time you create an effective story, you must:

- Identify your primary audience.
- Focus on the overall message.
- Outline the core drama.
- Make it personal.
- Practice delivering it.

Let's explore how to execute each one together.

Identify Your Primary Audience

Before you start crafting your story, you should have clarity on who your primary audience is. What is this group's mindset and knowledge base on the content? Do you want the people in the group to be excited, curious, fearful, apprehensive, or charged up? How much do they know about your story already? Do they have any preconceived notions? If you don't have full awareness about your audience, you could craft a compelling story that misses the mark with those you are trying to reach.

Focus on the Overall Message

Just about every great story has an overarching message, moral, or key takeaway. Think of any of your favorite movies. There are many subplots, but they tend to be connected to one larger dominating theme. In *Star Wars,* the Rebels beat the Empire and destroyed that darn Death Star the enemy kept rebuilding. In *E.T.,* Elliott and helpers made sure to get the poor fellow back home. Think of the story you want to tell your employees.

If being risk averse is a core concern within your organization, you might focus on how taking risks and embracing failure is essential for long-term success as the major guiding thought. If the key concern is speed and adapting to a rapidly changing competitive environment, the ability to collaborate, transcend silos, and work differently might be your guiding thought.

Outline the Core Drama

Any great story has a core drama that shapes its narrative. Whether it's something that disrupts, creates a new challenge, or forces the key characters to think and act differently, drama is present.

Be clear on that drama and make it a critical component of your narrative. This could be a nontraditional competitive threat, the inability to work together within the organization, or a dramatic shift in customer expectations. No matter the situation, you will want to build out that core drama element and channel most energy toward overcoming that issue.

Make It Personal

Every story gains credibility and authenticity when it feels real and personal. So if you think that changes in customer expectations are a real threat to how you can compete, share personal experiences that friends, family, or even you personally experienced when purchasing your product or service. This might create unexpected "aha" moments.

We were working with the CEO of a leading building products company that had great products but was struggling with the customer experience it provided. At a leadership meeting, the CEO shared a detailed account of how he remodeled his kitchen and the very frustrating experience he had buying his cabinets and said that he was inclined never to do it again. It made the challenge more vivid and personal, and it moved the topic from an intellectual customer experience problem to a meaningful account of what it is like to interact with the company's products and channels in real life.

Practice Delivering It

Interestingly, when we ask leaders how often they practice giving a keynote speech or a key presentation to their board, they respond by saying, "Always." When we then ask how often they practice telling their strategy story to their people, their answer is, "Rarely."

Like most things in life, it takes practice to be great. In boxing, the conventional wisdom is that you have to practice for 30,000 minutes to be good for 3. Comedians run through an incredible amount of reps before they master the timing of their jokes. As leaders, we often share content in real time and don't practice our delivery. The ability to practice how you tell your story, where to emphasize certain points, where to pause for reflection, and how to really engage with your audience simply takes time and practice.

Putting These Steps into Action

By combining these story creation essentials (primary audience, overarching message, core drama, making it personal, and practice), you will have a storyline that complements your vision headline. So next time you are preparing to share your strategy story with your people, take your strategy PowerPoint deck and consider using the template in Figure 2.3 as a guide to help you turn it into a compelling story.

OUR STRATEGY STORY

Vision statement:

Your overarching storyline:

Where are we coming from that is providing us the opportunity to be here today? *(This looks at our past strengths and accomplishments that have shaped our journey.)*

Core drama: What in our world is changing that is shaping our story? *(This is the story of how your environment is being shaped by technology; regulatory, competitive, or customer trends; or internal challenges.)*

What are we excited to create in the future that allows us to stay ahead of the curve and win? (Key strategies)
Examples:
– How are our customers profoundly better off with us than they are without us?
– How are we more agile or effective internally?

What do we need to watch out for that could cause us to stumble on our journey?

What change does it require from each of us?

How do we know we are winning?

FIGURE 2.3   *"Our Strategy Story" template*

Finding the right language that connects with your audience is not easy, and even the all-time greats can struggle with it. There is a fantastic story captured in *Time* about Martin Luther King Jr. at the beginning of the civil rights movement.

On August 28, 1963, 250,000 people participated in the March on Washington to bring attention to and build momentum for the civil rights movement. It was also the day when Dr. King gave his famous "I Have a Dream" speech. But at the outset, things were actually not going all that well.

Dr. King had planned to deliver a speech about policy to be sure he shared all the information on where the movement would go from here. Shortly after he began, it was clear that the crowd was starting to lose interest. Dr. King started to go off script, and as he did so, gospel singer and friend Mahalia Jackson leaned in and said, "Tell 'em about the dream, Martin." That inspired him to share with us a dream that shaped the path of the civil rights movement and our national psyche as much as any speech of the twentieth century.

Not all speeches or moments put you in front of 250,000 people or at the epicenter of a huge social movement. But once Dr. King started sharing his dream of what he envisioned the future to look like, he captured the imagination, energy, and passion of the crowd. And the rest is history.[4] As you think about the story you want to tell, be sure to use language that will resonate with your audience intellectually and emotionally, versus writing for yourself. You want the people you are addressing to get excited and inspired by your ideas.

YOUR ABILITY TO SHARE YOUR STORY EFFECTIVELY AS A LEADER

Having a compelling strategy story does not mean you are good at sharing it. Let's assume you now have a great vision statement and a compelling strategy story supporting it. What can get in the way now? The answer is the ability of your leaders to convey it effectively.

The gap between leaders thinking they are effective at telling the story and what the rest of the organization thinks is pretty stunning. After leaders give a presentation, we often witness human resources or communications folks high-fiving about how well the message was delivered. When we then ask people within the organization how they felt about what was shared and what stuck, we get an entirely different story.

Addressing this gap provides tremendous opportunity for better engagement of your people and effective activation of your strategic ambition.

Your "telling a great story" goal should be to have a three- to five-minute story that is your own, that you can tell with passion and conviction, and that inspires people to connect with the larger ambitions of the organization. From there, you can build out your story based on need, audiences, or length of time you have.

In Tim Pollard's fantastic read *The Compelling Communicator*,[5] he writes:

> It's surprising to me how often presenters know they
> have built a poor presentation, but somehow manage to
> persuade themselves that it does not really matter . . .
> they decide to simply apologize for the shortcomings
> rather than taking the time to go back and correct it. "I
> know you can't read this slide," "I know I am making you
> drink from the firehose," "If you don't mind me running
> long, let me take a few extra minutes to get through this"
> are all-too-common explanations we've heard and sins
> we likely committed. This simply DOES NOT WORK
> and it actually undermines the credibility of the message
> AND the leader.

As Pollard shows in his book, when a leader or senior executive delivers a poor presentation, 83 percent of listeners develop a moderate or significantly negative perception of that person's overall leadership ability. That is impact far beyond how good a storyteller you are. That is impact on how effective you will be as a leader. Period.

Not too long ago, we were in a session with the executive team of a large global financial firm that was going through significant change. We spent more than two days working through several hundred pages of a presentation created by one of the world's most renowned strategy consulting firms to determine how the organization needs to respond in a world of newly emerging financial technology firms and rapidly changing customer expectations. New strategies, new ways of serving the customer, new leadership, and new processes were all part of the change. The goal was to determine how the organization needed to evolve to maintain and expand its leadership. We had great dialogue, and the team landed on new strategies and structures that would profoundly impact the organization and people's jobs for years to come.

For the last half day of the retreat, we took a step back, looked at the tremendous volume of work, and tried to create the story of what was happening for the entire organization. Why are we changing, what does winning look like for us as a company going forward, and how do we bring this change to life to continue to be a leader in our industry?

To start the activity, we broke the executives into two teams and gave them 60 minutes to work through the overall narrative and create a 3-minute story. The task was addressing the company's 10,000+ employees and making the case for why this change was necessary and exciting and something everyone would want to be a part of.

Now this is a very bright set of executives who are running an excellent company. They have all the right degrees, global experience, and a track record of success. They were also fully engaged in this challenge and working through the storyline.

As both teams gave their pitch, the CEO sitting next to us gave us a funny look and then leaned over and whispered, "These stories suck. I would not get out of bed in the morning and be excited about this."

This was astounding, as these people all worked through the critical strategic challenges, achieved alignment, were fully on board with the overall direction, and were excited to tell the story to the rest of the organization. And even with those requirements present, their stories did anything but inspire.

Think about your story; make sure it is compelling, clear, and understandable and be sure that success is defined when you see the energy and passion that you have for the subject in the faces of your people. Let's now explore the difference between using common words and achieving true shared meaning of our story.

ACHIEVING SHARED MEANING OF YOUR STORY BY YOUR LEADERS

We've all heard the saying "A picture is worth a thousand words." We have found that to be exceedingly true in business. As a matter of fact, the right use of visualization is one of the most effective ways to align leaders on critical business issues and achieve shared meaning.

Words

We had the opportunity to work with a global chemical company, and one of the objectives was to capture the story of the company's strategy so we could engage the larger organization more effectively in it. The change required restructuring of the organization itself and was impacting a lot of people. It was critical to clearly outline the why, what, and how of the change to employees. And it was essential that all team members had a clear sense of why this was happening, why they should want to be on this journey, and how they could contribute in the best way.

We had an interview session with the CEO as well as the head of strategy where we rigorously took notes to capture our discussion. Then we returned to our offices and spent time with one of our concept artists to work through the story and capture the essence as we heard it. Armed with a tight outline and a sketch that we felt good about, we returned to the CEO and head of strategy a few days later. After we revealed the sketch and shared our version of the story, both of them looked at the sketch for an extended period of time, quietly absorbing it. Then the dialogue went something like this:

> **CEO**: I am not sure you were fully listening to me or you understood our strategy because you really missed the essence here.
>
> **Head of strategy**: I actually think it's quite good, and it really captures the story we have been talking about.
>
> **CEO**: No, it doesn't. It doesn't capture the essence of the shift and ultimately our strategy really well.
>
> **Head of strategy:** Well, I think this represents exactly what you said.
>
> **CEO**: One thing is for sure: If that is what I said, it is not what I meant. It doesn't convey it the right way.

Let's allow that to sink in for a moment: "If that is what I said, it is not what I meant."

Aligning what you say and what that means in your head and conveying that exact message to someone else is quite hard. Aligning on words is easy. Aligning on the meaning behind those words to have a common story or view of the system is very different.

Let's illustrate through a different example. Close your eyes for a second and draw a *detailed* picture in your head of what comes to mind when you read the word "hometown."

No, really. Do it.

What did you see? The town you grew up in? The town you live in now? A city? A small town? A suburb?

What experiences shaped this image for you? Was it where you spent the most time in your life? Where most of your relatives live?

If you asked five of your colleagues to draw a similar picture in their heads of the word "hometown," how different or similar do you think it would look? Chances are your answer won't be the same as anyone else's because the word "hometown" is associated with a wide range of meanings and emotions for people. This goes for most words. We associate different imagery and meanings in our heads with the same words all the time, and that is what gets our stories to significantly diverge when we tell them.

Think of words that we commonly use when talking about our strategies—words like "growth," "customer focus," "innovation," "leverage," "synergies," "collaboration," or "leadership." We likely agree on the word itself, but when we ask others to draw the meaning and what it really looks or feels like in action, the pictures are often as different as the images we draw of our hometowns.

Visualization

It's also important to note that our brain has the ability to process complex information and give it meaning a lot faster visually than through the written word. So the question is really: Why don't we use visualization more often when explaining complex things? The data is obvious—visuals are the superior way to achieve shared meaning.

Robert E. Horn, a renowned scholar who has taught at Harvard, Columbia, and Stanford, might have said it best at a National Science Foundation meeting when he stated that "visual language has the potential for increasing 'human bandwidth'—the capacity to take in, comprehend, and more efficiently synthesize large amounts of new information."

Shared meaning ensures that our story goes beyond common words but has a much deeper sense of shared understanding, alignment, and ultimately meaning to people. Doing this effectively is the difference between people partially understanding your story and not getting in the way of it and you owning your story and being an advocate for it.

How might you use visualization to create shared meaning without an artist or designer in the room? Consider the many times when you have witnessed people trying to get their ideas across by drawing images, arrows, or word pictures on a napkin to express in detail something that they were excited about—or when you have done the same thing yourself. You can use the same approach to begin to visualize your story. Try the steps in Figure 2.4.

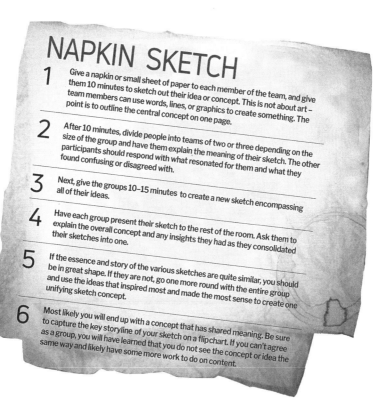

NAPKIN SKETCH

1 Give a napkin or small sheet of paper to each member of the team, and give them 10 minutes to sketch out their idea or concept. This is not about art – team members can use words, lines, or graphics to create something. The point is to outline the central concept on one page.

2 After 10 minutes, divide people into teams of two or three depending on the size of the group and have them explain the meaning of their sketch. The other participants should respond with what resonated for them and what they found confusing or disagreed with.

3 Next, give the groups 10–15 minutes to create a new sketch encompassing all of their ideas.

4 Have each group present their sketch to the rest of the room. Ask them to explain the overall concept and any insights they had as they consolidated their sketches into one.

5 If the essence and story of the various sketches are quite similar, you should be in great shape. If they are not, go one more round with the entire group and use the ideas that inspired most and made the most sense to create one unifying sketch concept.

6 Most likely you will end up with a concept that has shared meaning. Be sure to capture the key storyline of your sketch on a flipchart. If you can't agree as a group, you will have learned that you do not see the concept or idea the same way and likely have some more work to do on content.

FIGURE 2.4 *Napkin sketch*

Visual thinking is a great accelerator to understand and align on concepts. The activity in Figure 2.4 is an effective and fun way to make rapid progress toward achieving shared meaning of your story.

If you have created a great vision with a compelling strategy story, are comfortable sharing that story, and have shared meaning around that with your team, you have addressed a critical blind spot. But we're sorry to inform you that you're not out of the woods.

In the next chapter we'll explore why most good stories die without having a major impact.

CHAPTER THREE

Leadership Blind Spot #3:
ENGAGEMENT

Common Misconception

*Rational and logical presentations engage
the hearts and minds of people.*

The Basics

*In many organizations, a tremendous amount of money
is spent creating strategies to win. Those strategies then get
communicated using PowerPoint presentations, road shows,
or town hall meetings—but things seemingly get stuck. Employees fail
to connect with the strategy, leaders are frustrated about the lack of
progress, and managers just try to hold the ship together.*

The Question We Will Answer

*How do we move from presentations to conversations and create
genuine engagement in strategies in the business?*

WHAT DOES IT FEEL LIKE
TO BE SOLD AND TOLD?

Just recently, one of us attended an Amy Grant concert at a performing arts center. The center combined the renovation of an amazing historical landmark with the addition of the latest acoustic technology. To make it even more impressive, the concert hall had a lush look of gold detailing, marble imagery, crystal chandeliers, and paintings that evoked some of the most memorable concert halls in Vienna. The hall would only seat 1,000 people for the concert, and while almost every seat was taken at this small Indiana university, the venue still had a sense of intimacy, as there wasn't a bad seat in the house. It was a warm summer evening, and we were excited to see this six-time Grammy award winner perform.

Right on cue at 8 p.m., a four-piece band walked out onto the stage, and the musicians took their seats. A man in a sport coat followed out on stage to kick things off. Our assumption was that he was going to introduce the band. That is not exactly what happened. He proceeded to talk about an upcoming event at the center and the tickets that were on sale for a visiting symphony. He talked about how good the orchestra was last year, where he sat with his grandchildren, how to purchase the tickets, and that if you didn't move soon, you might be left out. All good and nice, but you could hear the audience get restless as his 5 minutes turned into 10, and he just kept on talking. It was like a movie theater where the previews never seem to end. Just when we thought he was finally done, a screen came down on stage, and he started showing pictures of last year's performance. Phones started coming out, and the crowd grew truly restless, and you could hear the elevated chatter that you get in a bigger room when no one is paying attention to anything in particular.

When he finally said, "Well, you didn't come here to hear me talk, so . . . ," before he could finish his sentence, the crowd started to applaud, and the applause only got louder as he left the stage. The message was clear that we don't like being sold tickets for the next event when we came to enjoy this one.

How could someone be so out of touch with the audience? How could he have such a blind spot about how people felt as his remarks dragged on?

Sadly, we see this type of engagement in company settings all the time. The challenge is that many leaders have a similar blind spot when it comes to engaging their people. Some go-to techniques often generate the same feeling as the man with the mic at the Amy Grant concert, and no leaders want a standing ovation when they are finally done speaking because their content and comments don't resonate with their people—who are happy for them to get off the stage.

THE DOUBLE P

In a business setting, we frequently see similarly tone-deaf presentations when executives use an overabundance of slides to tell a story and engage their people. However, Edward R. Tufte, a professor emeritus of political science, computer science, and graphic design at Yale, has an interesting perspective on leaders, their blind spots, and the tools they use to engage their people. Tufte pulls no punches when he suggests that "PowerPoint is evil," and he uses a pharmaceutical example to back up his assertion that power corrupts and PowerPoints corrupt absolutely.

Tufte suggests that we imagine a highly touted drug that promised to make us beautiful but didn't deliver. Instead the drug had frequent and serious side effects—such as fostering stupidity, wasting time, creating confusion, turning important topics into boring ones, telling a story poorly, and even inducing middle-of-the-day drowsiness. Tufte argues that in the pharma world, these negative side effects would undoubtedly lead to a worldwide product recall.

As Tufte so aptly puts it, "Slideware may help speakers outline their talks, but convenience for the speaker can be punishing to the story, content, and the experience of the audience. The standard PowerPoint presentation elevates format over content and turns everything into a sales pitch."[1] This, in turn, sets up the speaker's dominance over the audience, where you feel like you are being sold something that you wouldn't buy if you had the choice.

The reality is that we use presentations every day to tell stories, share data, pitch ideas, and try to connect with our people. But there is one problem: Most of the time we do a terrible job connecting with an audience and accomplishing what we set out to do. Sadly, our presentations largely fail to invigorate our people to challenge the way they currently think about their role, their contributions to the organization, and their behaviors that need to change.

From what we have had the privilege to observe, in real life these types of presentations are received with the edge-of-your-seat enthusiasm you see in Figure 3.1.

FIGURE 3.1 *One-way presentations fail to engage people.*

It is not just that boring presentations create an instant adverse reaction—it is the blind spot that leaders have that suggests we can present our way into the hearts and minds of our people.

WHAT DOES ENGAGEMENT LOOK LIKE TO OUR PEOPLE?

We know that executive incentives are based on improving employee engagement scores and that the primary focus for many leaders is often getting better numbers, and not addressing the real issues that we know drive engagement.

So what really drives engagement? A recent *Harvard Business Review* article, titled "The 3 Things Employees Really Want: Career, Community, Cause," reveals three categories of motivators that employees value most when it comes to engagement at work. These areas include:

- **Intrinsic motivation.** Being able to use their strengths along with the opportunity to learn and grow.
- **Connectedness and belonging.** Having a sense of being respected, recognized, and cared about by others.
- **Pride.** Identifying with the organizational mission, and feeling they make an impact in bringing that mission to life.[2]

Here at Root Inc. we like to define engagement as the emotional commitment that people have to their team, the organization, and the strategies of their company. Being emotionally committed means employees really care about and are invested in their work and in the success of their organization. In many ways, it is the reciprocal "care relationship" between people and their organization that creates true engagement.

Emotionally Connecting to Change

Interestingly, *Change or Die* author Alan Deutschman explains that "the secret is to move away from presenting or marketing to our people with the old pitch of **force** (we have to change), **facts** (it's obvious why we should change), and **fear** (bad things will happen if we don't change)—and replace it with relationships that inspire hope."[3]

In our experience, relationships of hope can only be developed from authentic conversations rather than well-scripted presentations. Deutschman proposes that all leadership comes down to changing people's behavior. He suggests that the traditional approach to change has a foundational belief that, as leaders, we can rationally instruct our people to change and that they will do it! And after 25 years in the field working with many of the greatest companies on the planet, we can say with certainty that Alan's research is accurate—it simply does not work.

We have found that the employee road shows, town halls, video talks, and cafeteria chats are usually built to be well-rehearsed, direct, tell-and-sell events that represent a one-way street of cascading information. Organizations think, "If we say it often enough, surely people will do what we want them to do." While people typically won't resist the change, they will have a huge and instant resistance to being changed by someone else. And this resistance goes up a notch when leaders suggest that people must become more urgent in the way they go about rapidly and comprehensively executing the business changes that leadership is suggesting.

One reason that the "force, facts, and fear" approach that Deutschman explains isn't effective is that it fails to acknowledge the principle of emotional intelligence, which is the true control center for human engagement and change. Each of us strongly safeguards the personal change control room and determines when to open it and when to keep it closed. When the three Fs are used, people comply in the short term but don't have real ownership of the change. It is obedience rather than authentic self-motivation or engagement.

As leaders, we tend to think people are rational, and we approach our people with a rational mindset. The assumption is that if you give people accurate and succinct information, they will make the right decisions and change. But that is not the reality. Extensive research has shown that the most successful change takes place when leaders emotionally connect with their people and inspire a new sense of hope.

In partnering with Global 2000 clients as they attempt to motivate their people to "buy into" their change agenda, it has become clear that *employee motivation is personal, and commitment to change cannot flow from a leader's lips to an employee's head and heart!* For the motivation, ownership, advocacy, and risk taking associated with change to come to life, an openness and excitement for change must come from an experience that changes the way employees see their business, their organization, and their role in it.

Solving Our Own Puzzles

In speaking to various leadership groups, we often ask the audience to respond to a few questions on engagement. We start by asking people to identify areas of their life where they are truly engaged. We typically get answers such as dinner conversations, sporting events, games, and stories.

We then go a little deeper and ask how many people are fans of crossword puzzles or sudoku, are true gamers, and/or love to read novels, and a majority of hands go up. Each of these hobbies has the attraction and engagement power to hold people's attention for hours.

The next question we ask goes like this: "How many of you look at the answer key before starting a sudoku puzzle, read blogs with cheats on how to win a video game, or read the last chapter of a novel first?" Sure, there is always that one person who can't help doing it, but the others in the room keep their hands down.

When we ask the leaders in the audience, "Why not?" they respond with indignation. They say that it is not challenging or fun because you aren't testing how good you are and there is no sense of achievement. Comments such as "It would be boring" or "Why bother?" are heard often as well.

Then we ask these same leaders how they think their people must feel when they are given the answers to execute a strategy. Not surprisingly, they quickly make the connection and acknowledge that they're taking away challenges and excitement from their people—not to mention a feeling of inclusion by working with other people on their teams to find solutions.

By being aware of how you may be contributing to disengagement and stifling inspiration, you're becoming one step closer to seeing through this blind spot.

So what's next?

Having Authentic Conversations

Understanding and appreciating that authentic, dialogue-rich conversations are required to enable change is a crucial way to resolve Blind Spot #3. Dialogue is at the root of all effective engagement and the only pathway to authentically engage the hearts and minds of people.

After 25 years of observing people at every level of organizational life (from the front line to the senior team), we can say that there is one observation in particular that is a game changer when it comes to any leader's assumptions and beliefs about employee engagement: *people will tolerate the conclusions of their leaders, but they will only act on their own conclusions.*

If we don't create the environment and conditions that will allow our people to examine, consider, challenge, rethink, and end up with new observations and conclusions about the business, then engagement, execution, and change will not happen. However, when people have the opportunity to engage in conversations that share the essential drama of the business (such as threats and opportunities) and are invited to co-think actions that can be taken to address both, they are invigorated. They feel that they play a major role in contributing to the success of their team and the company.

We are often asked how a leader can start these conversations. What does the environment look like? Is there a right time or wrong time to have these conversations? We often suggest that leaders repeat a process with their people that leadership teams tend to go through in order to frame new strategies, critical priorities, or initiatives. We simply suggest that leaders repeat their own personal thinking journey with their people. Once the specific questions under the categories of "why" we need to change, "what" we need to change to, and "how" we will execute our changes are brainstormed and prioritized, they should be used both to engage your people to co-think the critical changes necessary in the business and to help people understand their role in executing these changes.

Below we review in more detail the types of questions that best help people co-think the overall business. The organizations that truly understand the relationship between authentic conversations and results will typically hold authentic conversation sessions with their people every quarter throughout the organization. However, innovative organizations are finding ways to literally have these conversations every day.

In his book, *Dialogue and the Art of Thinking Together,* William Isaacs suggests that "few practices seem to lie more at the heart of human communities than talking and telling stories."[4] He explains that ancient Greeks saw *dia logos*, or flow of meaning, as the cornerstone of pride and self-governing. Isaacs further observes that "the problems that even the most practical organizations have in improving performance and obtaining the results they desire can be directly traced to their inability to think and talk together, particularly at critical moments." We couldn't agree more. As we have watched organizations of all shapes and sizes deal with accelerating change and increasing ambiguity, they have struggled to get smart about how their people think together as organizations, groups and teams.

When we worked with the new senior team of two large merging companies, the CEO kept suggesting that they were speaking *at* each other, and in his words, "Even more troubling, we are speaking *past* each other." It wasn't dialogue. It was a rapid-fire monologue. He suggested that they were, at best, engaged in cross talk and that they really didn't know how to engage one another in authentic conversation. He lamented that they hadn't learned essential and basic communication skills. These included listening to one another, bringing unexamined assumptions out in the open, landing on common ground for key issues, identifying the best ways to explore innovative ideas and perspectives, and most importantly, arriving at a place of shared meaning on the most critical issues for the new company. He further said, "We lack the know-how and tools to do this well."

If authentic conversations are the solution, leaders need to begin creating environments in which employees can discuss, examine, and rethink how authentic conversations can positively change beliefs, opinions, and attitudes.

So how do we start these conversations? How do we demystify dialogue? How do we craft employee-led dialogue as a living experience of inquiry within and between people?

We must create an environment for dialogue-rich conversation by focusing on both a "Model for Dialogue" and the "Principles for Orchestrating Great Conversations." Doing so will result in true inquiry and the ability for your people to think together.

The Model for Dialogue

The Model for Dialogue is helpful to think about as the sequence or outline to follow for harnessing the collective intelligence of the people around you. Thinking together implies that each of us relaxes our grip on certainty in order to explore different assumptions, beliefs, opinions, and conclusions.

We have found that the Model for Dialogue includes three areas: context, content, and application. These areas for conversation help set the stage for critical thinking for individuals and groups. Almost any issue can be structured to logically progress through these three areas and bring people to a new level of shared understanding and meaning.

Let's dive into each:

1. **Context.** Context is often thought of as the big picture. Dialogue that harvests the collective wisdom of an organization, group, or team must start with the context, or big picture. This helps everyone connect the dots and have the ability to associate one idea with another. Big-picture dialogue often helps frame the "why" behind actions or inactions and is especially helpful in enabling people to understand and think in systems. Big-picture dialogue questions often look like this for businesses and teams:
    - What are the major trends that will be affecting us the most in the future?
    - What big-picture issues are we least prepared for?
    - What are the top three to five keys to our future success?
    - What are our overall strengths and weaknesses?

2. **Content.** Content is often the change we are focusing on. It could be a new strategy, process, way of thinking or behaving, or improvements that we have prioritized in the overall

business plan. Content dialogue often starts with understanding the content, identifying how it addresses the big-picture challenges, painting a clear picture of the strategy story, and addressing what winning looks like. Content dialogue questions often look like this:

- How would you describe what we are trying to build for our customers and our people?
- What does winning look like for our organization and our people?
- Where will we focus and target our efforts to bring our winning aspirations to life?
- How will we go about winning?

3.   **Application.** Application is all about tapping the experience, knowledge, creativity, and talents of our people to solve the problems and create opportunities that context and content questions set up. The following questions can be used to explore ideas for innovation and successful change:

- How can we best achieve our strategic goal of becoming a low-cost producer of products and services?
- Where are the greatest opportunities for enhancing collaboration between sales and operations?
- How can we make important information available to our business partners quicker?
- Where should we focus our efforts to build a market-leading customer experience for our customers?
- What skills and capabilities must we have to be successful?

In our experience, creating a line of sight "from the marketplace to me" for everyone in the organization occurs when dialogue is focused on the *context* (the why of change), *content* (the what of change), and *application* (the how of change).

Principles for Orchestrating Great Conversations

Creating an organization that embraces dialogue takes a proactive and thoughtful approach. What follows are several principles that will help you get started.

So how do we change the recurring leader habit of directing, telling, and trying to sell our people to buy into our new strategy and to behave differently? One way is changing the way we look at dialogue. Daniel Yankelovich, author of *The Magic of Dialogue,* suggests that dialogue is "creating shared understanding in an atmosphere of mutual respect and support to arrive at a mutually beneficial outcome."[5] Instead of looking at a conversation as an exchange of information, think of it as a process of creating shared meaning. As Yankelovich suggests, it is only in creating shared meaning between people that we have the possibility to solve the challenges we face.

If you are looking for ways to create more of a dialogue culture, some of the most effective strategies include Socratic questioning, small-group conversations, and the use of visuals and data to drive inquiry and understanding.

Socratic Questions   First and foremost, when looking to co-think about the most important issues of your business, you must use Socratic questioning. Socratic questioning is harder than it sounds. You wouldn't believe how many times questions that are intended to be open-ended, probing, and thinking questions end up being thinly disguised closed-ended questions.

So what is Socratic questioning exactly? Socratic questioning is a way to explore complex ideas, open up problems, uncover assumptions, connect relationships, and analyze concepts. Socratic questioning is systematic, disciplined, and useful to probe thinking. Socrates believed that questioning is the only defensible form of teaching and that it helps students begin to distinguish what they know or understand from what they do not know or understand, all with a goal of developing intellectual humility in the process.

A key to engaging people in Socratic questions is believing your people are capable of having great conversations and uncovering even better answers than we could script for them. By asking effective questions, you let the knowledge and experiences of your people drive the conversation and the experience, which is the missing link for true engagement and true change.

Here are several Socratic questions we have seen that generate successful conversations. They prompt thinking and do not have right or wrong answers.

- Why do you say that?
- What would be an example?
- What would be an alternative?
- What are your observations?
- How does this relate to our major concerns?

True Socratic dialogue is based on asking questions to encourage critical thinking. This will then draw out presumptions and underlying assumptions so they can be challenged and addressed.

Some of the most difficult business issues we face today are too complex to be solved by one person. Dialogue seeks to harness the collective intelligence of the people in the organization. The greatest leaders are teachers, and great teachers are masters of questions. The Socratic method inspires and trains employees to be inquisitive and accountable, and often it is the key for people to evolve from apathy and indifference about their business to insightful urgency about what needs to change.

Small-Group Conversations   Think about different dinner conversations you have had in the past. As the numbers at your table get larger, it is hard to have one conversation, and more often than not,

According to a recent Nationwide survey:

MORE DOCTORS SMOKE CAMELS
THAN ANY OTHER CIGARETTE

DOCTORS in every branch of medicine—113,597 in all—were queried in this nationwide study of cigarette preference. Three leading research organizations made the survey. The gist of the query was—What cigarette do you smoke, Doctor?

The brand named most was Camel!

The rich, full flavor and cool mildness of Camel's superb blend of costlier tobaccos seem to have the same appeal to the smoking tastes of doctors as to millions of other smokers. If you are a Camel smoker, this preference among doctors will hardly surprise you. If you're not—well, try Camels now.

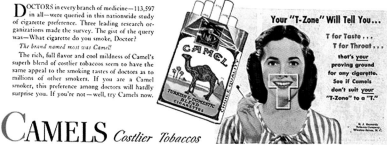

Your "T-Zone" Will Tell You...

T for Taste . . .
T for Throat . . .

that's your proving ground for any cigarette. See if Camels don't suit your "T-Zone" to a "T."

CAMELS *Costlier Tobaccos*

Figure I.3

Figure I.4

Figure 1.3

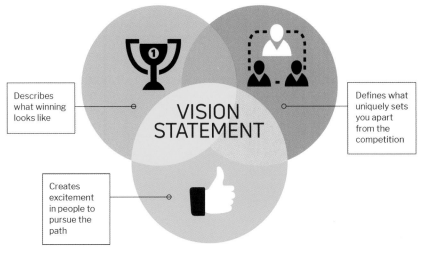

Describes what winning looks like

Defines what uniquely sets you apart from the competition

Creates excitement in people to pursue the path

VISION STATEMENT

Figure 2.2

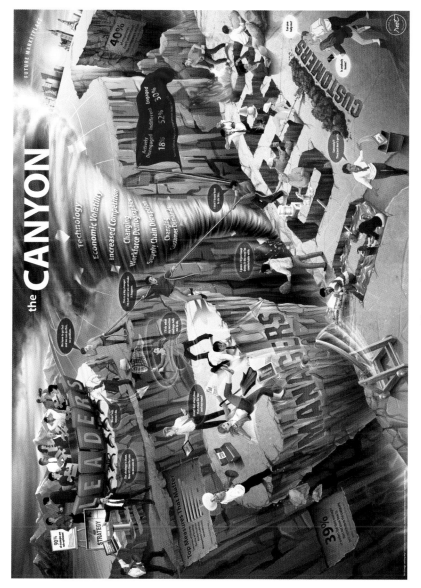

Figure 3.4

Figure 3.5

Figure 3.6

Figure 3.7

the table seems to break up into a number of smaller conversations as the group grows.

We have found that the optimal number for great dialogue is 8 to 10 people. This number allows all the members of the group to have a voice while also allowing them to feel safe to express what they truly think and feel. In thousands of small-group dialogue debriefs, participants have told us that when they are with their peers in small groups, they are least fearful of suggesting the wrong answer or being embarrassed and most willing to explore and reach for new insights.

A recent Edelman Trust Barometer revealed that one person in three doesn't trust the company for which he or she works, but the person's peers represent the category of people that the person most trusts. Having a trusting environment is necessary for success. In Figure 3.2, you can see an example of people in a small group having strategic conversation.

FIGURE 3.2 *Small-group dialogue centered around a visual and data*

Visuals and Data   While Socratic questions, pursued in small-group dialogue, can help create important discoveries that give way to new learning, innovative ideas, and new behaviors, setting the stage for dialogue with data and visuals is also a catalyst to great dialogue. Data and pictures create a mental practice field or brain gym to focus the dialogue that will take place. They encourage big-picture and system thinking. This data can be infographics, a single chart, or even a dynamic metaphor. Whatever it is, it must capture multiple factors that help form a connected story to discuss.

Figure 3.3 shows a simple example of pricing trends compared with inflation for a consumer products company. This company wanted to take a strategic issue right to its front-line people. For this company, the critical conversation was around core product pricing strategy. Core product pricing had been lagging far behind inflation. However, the company experienced employee resistance to the number of new products that it was trying to introduce.

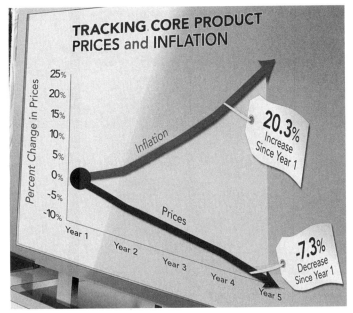

FIGURE 3.3   *A pricing trends chart provides data that becomes part of the dialogue.*

After being asked to "read the data on the chart and describe what you see," people engaged in discussing a series of questions that went like this:

- Why do you think the pricing for our core products has lagged so far behind inflation?
- Do you think we will be able to increase our pricing in the future? Why or why not?
- What do you think our closest competitors would do if we increased our prices?
- What do you think our consumers would do?
- What do you think we should do to address this reality?

The employee conversations went like this across the entire company:

"Our prices have lagged so far behind inflation because of intense and ever-improving competition and because consumers are increasingly finding better and healthier alternatives."

"If we increased our pricing, we would have a possible short-term positive bump, but we believe that our competition would not increase their prices and they would use this opportunity to steal market share that we would likely not get back."

"A price increase would also accelerate our customers' move to new, alternative products."

"It seems that given the fact that we will not get a wage increase from better pricing on our core products in the marketplace with our customers, we need to find new and innovative ways to bring new products to market, and when new products are introduced, do our best to make sure those product launches are as successful as possible."

More than a presentation ever could, the co-thinking of the pricing dilemma caused people to relax their grip on staying the course on just the core products and open up to the stream of new products being developed. Even more than being open to these new offerings, people on the front line continued to be curious about new-product introduction timing and would regularly discuss the best ways to develop customer interest and success.

Putting It All Together—Socratic Questions, Small Groups, and Visuals and Data   In our experience, dialogue-driven conversations are greatly enhanced when Socratic questions, small groups, and visuals and data are used together to enable system thinking.

While we were working with a large Canadian bank, the dialogue-rich conversations started slowly. After a brief time, voices raised a level or two with bold suggestions and ideas. The leaders were taken aback by the untapped intelligence, passion, and curiosity of their people, while the employees felt a profound sense of being valued by being invited to engage in a conversation about the future of the organization and their role in it.

One woman's comments after the conversation were memorable. She explained that this was the first time in 14 years at the bank that she had learned anything and told her leaders, "Everything that I was involved in was a one-way presentation to get me to do what you thought I should do."

She continued on and said something to her leaders that we have never forgotten: "You know, learning requires thinking, and this conversation is the first time that you didn't think for me and tell me what I should believe and how I should behave. It is the first time that you have asked me to co-explore, co-examine, and co-think how our business is changing. It is the first time I have examined what I thought to be true about retail banking today and where it is headed tomorrow."

What the people in the group discovered together caused them to change their conclusions about how the bank worked now and would work in the future. And once they changed their conclusions, it set the stage for them to change behaviors.

AN EVERYDAY EXAMPLE
OF THE POWER OF DIALOGUE

We often start our work with clients by getting them to think about the challenges that they face in effectively engaging and connecting their people to their business. We start the dialogue with a visual we call *The Canyon®*, a Root Learning Map® visual shown in Figure 3.4. The picture captures the organizational reality that many people feel and face every day, complete with drama, challenge, frustration, and true human perspectives on "the way things work around here." We invite people to use this picture of the current organizational realities to serve as a platform for dialogue-driven conversation.

FIGURE 3.4 *The Canyon®*

What have we found before and after introducing *The Canyon* with clients?

Before: Leaders had their eyes focused on the future and the key changes that needed to be undertaken, but they didn't have their hands directly on the day-to-day levers of change (Figure 3.5).

FIGURE 3.5   *The Leaders*

Doers had their hands on the levers of change but didn't have a clue what to do differently (Figure 3.6).

FIGURE 3.6   *The Doers*

Managers felt stuck in the middle as they desperately tried to interpret what leaders wanted and frantically tried to translate it into something useful for their people (Figure 3.7).

FIGURE 3.7   *The Managers*

Additionally, external changes ushered in a tornado-like force that added to the gaps between leaders, managers, and doers. Often, it was common to blame someone else for perpetuating the gaps and canyons. Leaders blamed managers and often said that they "don't get it." Managers blamed doers and said they "won't act." And managers and doers blamed leaders and said they "don't walk their talk."

And after: Instead of polarizing or fighting about who was to blame, the people experiencing *The Canyon* visual began to consider the predicaments of leaders, managers, doers, and customers. They often began to think of the organization as a system and looked at all the different perspectives, not just their own. They pondered the forces in the tornado of external change. There was an emotional connection to what they often saw, and more importantly, it validated how they felt. They immediately felt safe to identify the factors and forces in their organization that were most responsible for their canyons. They ultimately began to suggest what they could do to bridge the gaps between leaders, managers, doers, and customers.

The visual depiction of the reality showed how they felt, the questions launched a pursuit of shared inquiry, and the relationship that emerged from groups of 8 to 10 people in conversation collectively deciding what they wanted to do about the canyon ushered in a new spirt of creativity and accountability for finding a solution— look back at Figure 3.1.

Try This with Your Team

Now let's take a second look at *The Canyon*, but this time let's apply it to your organization and your issues. Start by having this dialogue with a small group of people from your organization:

1.   Look at *The Canyon* visual. What stands out to you?

2. Find the tornado representing external forces of change. Which ones do you believe are having the biggest impact on our organization?
3. What forces would you add to the tornado?
4. When you look at the chasm between managers and doers, what do you believe is most responsible for these gaps?
5. Where do you believe we have the most significant canyons in our organization?
6. What actions do you believe you can take to help bridge our organizational canyons?

Each time *The Canyon* visual has been used in small groups, supported by Socratic dialogue like the questions above, we have found that people at first might blame someone else for the chaos they face. However, people eventually experience a sense of shared vulnerability in recognizing that the canyon was created by everyone. They also realize that it will require everyone's collective efforts to bridge the chasms at each level of the organization.

The shared assessment of an organization's canyons begins to unlock the conclusions and behaviors of people in the organization because it makes an emotional impact by validating what they think, feel, and experience every day. We hear comments like, "This really depicts what it is like to work around here," or "It is about time we talk about the real issues that are holding us back," or "We are not on the same page because we are at different altitudes in the organization and see the world differently. We need to all be on the same page!"

Authentic conclusions emerge about the truth that we each hold as the keys to positive change.

INSPIRING AUTHENTIC ENGAGEMENT

Authentic engagement is created by one act: inviting our people to *co-think*. The dignity that people feel when their ideas and perspectives are valued, and the power that is unleashed when their discretionary effort is freely contributed, is an unparalleled competitive advantage for any organization.

Inviting your people to help solve the problems of your business begins with leaders believing in the immense creation capability of their people. Shifting your thinking from "I am the creator, and my people are the implementers" to "I know this business well, but so do my people, and I can learn from them if I really listen" will transform your organization. By unleashing the care, creativity, judgment, and discretion of your people, your business will yield results far superior to what is achieved by scripting what they need to do.

When people believe in an organization's purpose (why we do what we do), have a vision statement supported by a strong strategy story (what we want to create that doesn't yet exist), and are invited into a conversation that identifies the greatest challenges and opportunities, you will have an engaged workforce. Most people have the knowledge and desire to do the right thing—and they will do it much better if we let them rather than tell them.

CHAPTER FOUR

Leadership Blind Spot #4: **TRUST**

Common Misconception

People will not do the right thing unless you tell them what to do and hold them accountable to do it.

The Basics

Companies want and need to deliver great service to differentiate themselves, and the common belief is that the best way to deliver this is to create tight processes, scripts, and routines that minimize variability— to hold people and their behaviors to a strict policy and uniform standards. But that approach will never create consistent yet unique, differentiated, and personalized experiences that lead the market.

The Question We Will Answer

How can we trust and scale the unique human judgment, discretion, and care of our people, while at the same time having firm standards that we all share?

AS LEADERS, WE OFTEN
DON'T TRUST OUR PEOPLE

A real-life example of not trusting our people to do the right thing, scripting exactly what they should do, and the unintended consequences it can bring occurred in an experience we had with one of the largest restaurant chains in the world. We found ourselves involved in a deeply probing conversation with the senior team of the brand regarding why some top-performing restaurants could generate $2 million a year in revenue, while the average restaurants were only generating $1.2 million a year in revenue. And this was for restaurants in comparable demographic areas, so it was a true apples-to-apples comparison. With over 5,000 restaurants across the country, this represented a possible upside revenue opportunity that could easily exceed $1 billion. The potential financial prize was huge.

Our conversation eventually led to the topic of how this senior team operated the business. After some time of sharing candid and direct opinions, the team members came to several conclusions about the underlying beliefs they had about their people and how these beliefs drove their day-to-day behaviors, processes, and routines.

We created truth statements with the team. Creating truth statements is the process of capturing the set of underlying beliefs that leadership teams consciously or subconsciously use to run their business. The first statement these team members landed on when they looked squarely in the mirror was, "We claim that we are customer maniacs, but in the end, we are finance and control maniacs who don't trust our people would do the right thing for our customers and our business if we took the controls off."

This honest assessment was profound, as they acknowledged that the core operating belief they used to run the business was to create mechanisms that kept people from screwing up instead of creating conditions for their people and restaurants to thrive. The second—and even more poignant—truth statement was, "We are trying to protect our customers from our people by eliminating all human variability in the operation of our restaurants, as we don't trust that they would do the right things on their own."

The team admitted that all the operations were structured to direct, tell, and enforce upon the employees what they must do at every level of the organization. The approach was rationalized as the only way to scale performance and achieve brand consistency. But the more revealing comment was, "We just don't trust that our people have the judgment and discretion to make decisions that are best for our business." As a result, the operations people scripted the necessary behaviors for restaurant general managers on the best way to run a restaurant. They also scripted the routines and behaviors for the team members that the restaurant general manager led. The overwhelming feeling by corporate leaders was that they had to protect the brand by making sure everything was uniform. The main dashboard for the restaurants was a "rack-and-stack" chart that showed how each restaurant in each region performed, from best to worst, on several highly controlled categories of performance. Interestingly, most of these categories were on the cost side of the business, and only a few were on the customer experience side. Whenever any restaurant got outside the acceptable rack-and-stack range, store leadership would describe that they were, "getting whacked by the corporate executives to get back in line." This approach enabled consistency, but the price of consistency was potentially $800,000 less ($2 million versus $1.2 million) in annual revenue per average restaurant.

After some insightful research, the leadership team discovered that the middle-performing restaurants did indeed focus extensively on controls and compliance policies, just as they had been told. These restaurants made sure they hit their control numbers, regardless of the business. However, the high-performing restaurants went a bit off script and focused primarily on two things. The first of the two areas of focus was on developing people and allowing those "developed people" great leeway in making decisions that were best for their customers. The analysis showed that the high-performing restaurants used much more trust in engaging their people in the way that they operated the business. They were guided by the goal of delighting the customer and considered it the "North Star" for everyone to follow.

Second, the high-performing restaurants focused on growing revenue rather than being totally preoccupied with cost controls that dominated the focus of the average-performing restaurant. Managers and their people were encouraged to use their creativity to build relationships in the community to grow new customers and new revenue streams for the business. Rather than scripting how this should be done, the restaurants encouraged their team members to use their knowledge of the local community and their own ingenuity to create partnerships with groups in the geography near the restaurant.

One of the best examples of the difference between a high-performing restaurant and a mid-performing restaurant occurred in the way they addressed labor differently. In other words, there was a "control way" and a "trust way." The people, or staffing, cost of a restaurant represents one of the largest expense categories that must be managed effectively. If these costs exceed what was modeled for the overall business and planned for on a weekly basis, it could easily destroy the profitability of a restaurant. Each restaurant, based on size, was provided a labor model that scripted the exact allowable amount of labor that could be used to operate the business. The allowances for labor were nuanced on a monthly, weekly, and daily basis. The average restaurants strictly managed labor to these allocation numbers. In other words, if the weekly or monthly allowed labor hours were running higher than they should, the managers would reduce the staff levels for the upcoming weeks. And if they were running behind the allowed labor hours, they would bring people in so they could get more hours. They would do this regardless of the impact it would have on guests and on the revenue of the business. They "managed labor to a number." The goal was to make sure they didn't get in trouble for exceeding the allowable labor hours and labor cost per period. As a rule, these average-performing restaurants were rarely out of compliance with the monthly labor expense they were supposed to have. But they missed the opportunity to be staffed for business peaks and inevitably lost business during these rush periods. Control was maintained at all cost, or should we say, at the cost of the guest experience and the revenue opportunities of the restaurant.

In the high-performing restaurants, managers were not managing labor to a number. Instead they were focused on determining labor based on a forecast they would develop for the ebbs and flows of customer traffic for the business. They used labor control as a guide but focused their time, energy, and efforts on predicting customer flows by time of day, day of the week, and week of the month. They did this by reaching out to the community to build relationships with organizations like PTAs, sports teams, schools, and scouts. They tried to bring these groups into the restaurant when the restaurant had demand downtimes.

It was the creativity of the restaurant manager and her or his team that led to engagement with the broader community. They devised unique ways to support the neighborhood organizations with food and refreshments, and it resulted in a high-performance recipe.

In this case, managers weren't told how to reach out to community organizations to bring groups into the restaurants; instead they were encouraged to use their own creativity and knowledge of the community to extend the business of the restaurant beyond what walked in the door every day.

In many other high-performance organizations, we see leaders do three things in relation to control and trust:

1. **Make their priorities clear.** In the restaurant example, this was the overall importance of managing labor costs.
2. **Build the context of why that is important.** Out-of-control labor costs can be a primary reason why restaurants are not successful, and matching labor to business volume is critically important.
3. **Invite people to use their strengths**. In the restaurant case, leaders encouraged their teams to build relationships with their community groups and serve them during traditional downtimes for the restaurant.

In our restaurant example, once the leaders of the brand understood the difference between average- and high-performing restaurants, they made several key changes in the way they operated the business to take full advantage of building and trusting the capabilities of the restaurant general managers and their teams. These changes included shifting many of the managerial control responsibilities to technology, developing managers to understand how to best develop and lead teams to delight customers, and enlisting the creative skills of managers and their teams to go out into the community to build relationships that could grow the revenue of the restaurant. The approach worked, as the restaurant brand became one of the best restaurant growth stories over a 10-year period.

This modus operandi is more the rule than the exception. Many of the organizations we have worked with experience a similar struggle. When you mix legal and HR rules with a bias for control, the desire to "risk-mitigate" often becomes a dominating mindset in an organization. If you want to create an environment of trust that allows people to be the best version of themselves, you must be very conscious about the tone you set, because it does not happen by itself.

TRUST VERSUS CONTROL

As shown in Figure 4.1, the natural tendency of most leaders is to want to exert control over things to ensure results. It is based upon the fundamental premise that if things are clearly defined and if people just did as they were told we would be in fantastic shape. But that approach is almost guaranteed to not create extraordinary results because it does not unleash true human potential. In the broadest sense, trust and control are opposites. Trust is the expectation of a future behavior by another party without stepping in and directly controlling that party's actions, while control is the establishment of rules to ensure behavioral compliance. In Vladimir Lenin's words, "Trust is good, but control is better." However, the best way to run a business that includes people could be the reverse: "Control is good, but trust is better."

"WELL, FIRST, I FEEL LIKE YOU'RE TREATING ME LIKE A ROBOT."

FIGURE 4.1   *Leading with a control mindset creates lackluster underperformance.*

Speaker and business coach Henrik Kniberg comments that trust is more powerful than control. In fact, you indirectly get better control through trust, while you will never get trust from control.

He uses a traffic analogy as shown in Figure 4.2 as a metaphor to help illustrate the difference between trust and control. He suggests that you can have a four-way crossing that uses either a roundabout or an intersection controlled by a stoplight. The traffic signal intersection is central control, as the lights determine who gets to go, and there are very clear rules. If there is an accident, it is usually clear whose fault it is, and who ran the light can easily be determined.

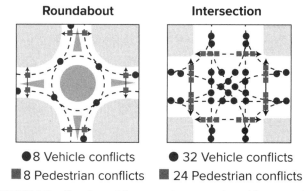

FIGURE 4.2   *Trust enables greater speed and less conflict.*

In the roundabout, the flow is based on trust and self-organization. People look around and make the decisions. There are no lights telling you when to go and stop. There are basic principles and a shared goal of safe navigation around the crossing.

The traffic circle seems chaotic, but it reduces the number of conflict points. In Kniberg's example, the roundabout only has 16 possible conflict points: 8 vehicles and 8 pedestrians. The intersection crossing with the stoplight has 56 points of conflict: 32 vehicles and 24 pedestrian ones. There is a large body of research that shows you get significantly faster flows through roundabouts and a lot fewer accidents.[1]

This is a useful analogy because a traffic circle is an excellent example of how trust can lead to better results. However, it doesn't work the other way, where controlling behavior leads to trust.

We have scientific evidence that roundabouts—or the concept of trusting people's judgment with some basic rules—are safer and more effective than the concept of completely controlling traffic flow with a traffic light. So why is it that we have such a tough time adopting that core philosophy in our workplaces? Why do we rely on control and rules over trust with guidance? Why don't we trust people to think and act on their own? Why do we like to control or script what we want our people to do? The single answer is that many organizations believe that you can't scale trust and that you can scale control. Just look at the number of policies and procedures that organizations put in place to make sure that there is consistency of process and experience. Let's examine an example that many of us are familiar with through this trust-versus-control lens and how it shapes culture and behavior.

United Airlines Flight 3411 Incident

On April 9, 2017, airport police at Chicago O'Hare International Airport forcibly removed passenger David Dao from Flight 3411 after he refused to give up his seat and leave the plane in an overbooked situation. The well-publicized experience of Dao being dragged off the plane, and apparently knocked unconscious with blood around his mouth, was recorded by fellow passengers, was posted on social media, and went viral. Outrage over the incident caused U.S. members of Congress to call for and hold hearings. Wikipedia created a special post titled "United Airlines Flight 3411 Incident." And over the course of the week following the incident, United stock fell 4 percent and reduced the company's market cap by $770 million.[2]

The horrible decision for United Airlines employees to call the police to remove a passenger from a Chicago to Louisville flight was predictable and years in the making, according to the opinion of a number of editorials written after the incident. Like most other airlines, United follows strict rules for handling passengers and has a culture where people are reluctant to make choices not in the book. It operates with a premise to put rules before people. It is this system of restrictions and permissions that allowed 69-year-old Dao to be dragged off the flight and end up in the hospital with a concussion, a broken nose, and two broken teeth.

In her book *Driving Excellence,* author Tara Allen suggests that an organization's culture can be defined in one of two ways:

1. To have a rules-based culture
2. To have a values-based culture

"What distinguishes a rules-based culture from a values-based culture is the degree of emphasis placed on trying to control or steer human thoughts and behaviors," Allen says. A rules-based approach emphasizes an extensive set of rules or a script to govern behavior. Certain industries, like airlines, utilities, or food service, understandably crave consistency to make sure that safety protocols are followed. Some rules are necessary. For example, safety in the cockpit with a preflight checklist is nonnegotiable. So are protocols on how to repair power lines in the utility industry and rules for preparation and storage measures for overall food safety in the food service industry.

In a values-based culture, according to Allen, the goal is to instill in the organization a common set of values that guide individuals' behaviors. The values are clearly stated and well defined to set the context for thinking and behaving. The organization is designed around what it holds as important, such as teamwork, customer experiences, innovation, continuous improvement, profitability, or purpose. Values-based cultures typically encourage more freedom and individual creativity and can have greater employee commitment and engagement.[3]

Allen points out that rules-based and values-based cultures both have their strengths and weaknesses and that healthy environments where people can thrive have the optimal blend of both. Rules-based environments drive conformity, whereas values-based approaches lead to freedom and empowerment. So how can we scale the unique human judgment, discretion, and care of our people while having firm standards that we all share?

The Answer Is in the "And"

In the words of Leonardo da Vinci, "Simplicity is the ultimate sophistication." The late cofounder of Apple, Steve Jobs, also had something to say relating to the importance of realizing simple is hard. He said, "Simple can be harder than complex: you have to work hard to get your thinking clean to make it simple." He followed up by saying, "But it's worth it in the end, because once you get there, you can move mountains." So is it possible to create an approach that utilizes both control and trust? Is it possible for leaders to be clear on areas that are nonnegotiable while also creating space for people to apply their own judgment, discretion, and care? It is, and the best leaders find a way to enable that.

In our experience, the best way to engage your people is to create an approach and a culture that has both control *and* trust and to make it as simple as possible for people to understand. Think about the "and" of control and trust as a complementary paradox. Consider the framework *to represent shared standards* or control, while freedom invites *individual creativity and discretionary effort* or trust.

The dangers of only control can be seen in organizations like United Airlines where the operating mindset can often be, "Human variability must be minimized so we can create conformity, predictability, scalability, and consistency." The focus is for people not to stray from the script, to uphold policies and avoid going outside the boundaries at all costs. It also presumes that the knowledge, discretion, and judgment that people have is inferior to a "company view" of what is necessary for a safe and consistent customer experience.

By scripting employees' responsibilities, holding them accountable for what's required, and rewarding the specific "scripted" behaviors, you can almost be sure of consistency. But at what cost? The problem isn't the occasional control freak; it's the hierarchical structure that systematically disempowers middle- and lower-level employees. The approach can virtually "forbid" employees from using their own best judgment. You would think in the United Airlines example that someone would stop the process and say that there must be a better way to get someone to vacate a seat, like upping the monetary offer, instead of hospitalizing the passenger who resisted—and paying a settlement that could have been a down payment on a future plane. In many situations like United's that call for some leeway, people feel they have no freedom to actively "own the situation." There are rules that simply can't be challenged, so they ignore their personal inclinations and cite "company policy."

We have seen many situations of businesses creating systems where employees don't feel trusted and therefore are contributing at the lowest common denominator possible. Think about it this way: As a consumer, you have the freedom to spend $20,000 or more on a new car. As an employee, you probably don't have the authority to requisition a $500 office chair. When you narrow people's scope of authority, you shrink their incentive to dream, imagine, and contribute.

Now, absolute freedom for employees to make decisions on their own without context or direction isn't the answer either. Standards for safety, quality, brand consistency, efficiency, and delivery of the expected products and customer experience all require common standards. The absence of these shared standards creates waste and reduces the confidence that customers have in any organization.

Let's go back to the same large restaurant system we discussed at the start of the chapter that operated primarily with a focus on controlling the cost components of a restaurant.

A previous CEO created a large amount of freedom in how restaurant general managers ran the stores and how the same store managers ran their districts. His belief was that corporate leadership should establish the most important outcomes and trust that well-intending people will decide how to achieve them. He believed trust alone could be relied on to get the results the brand and the guests were expecting. However, he became increasingly frustrated when customer feedback on "restaurant cleanliness" continued to fall far short of customer expectations. So he conducted a memorable experiment.

Prior to a regularly scheduled meeting of 30 district managers, he asked each manager to take two or three pictures of what a "clean restaurant" looked like to them. The CEO asked them to make sure that the pictures included the seating area, restaurant, restroom, and even the parking lot. He told them to bring these pictures to the meeting. One of the first tasks of the session was to tape more than 60 pictures of these "clean" restaurants on the wall.

It took about 30 seconds for most of the district managers to mumble, "Wow, we have a problem!" Some pictures showed spotless floors but clutter on the counter. Others had well-scrubbed dining rooms but haphazardly stacked supplies in the kitchen. And more than one picture showed organized and well-taken-care-of restaurants but parking lots with noticeable litter and trash that somehow didn't make it into the garbage cans. As a team, the district leaders agreed on the pictures that captured a comprehensive view of what cleanliness should look like for all restaurants and established the hard standards for appearance that all restaurants would strictly follow going forward.

In this situation, a consistent and hard framework for cleanliness was needed instead of the freedom for the managers to determine what "clean" looked like for their individual restaurants. A brief time after the agreed-upon visual standards for cleanliness were created and deployed, the customers' scores on cleanliness for the restaurant chain ascended to the expected level.

OPTIMIZING FRAMEWORK *AND* FREEDOM

To survive and thrive at an elevated level, leaders must create a culture that focuses on both framework *and* freedom. They must create a framework that clearly outlines the nonnegotiables that ensure consistency and safety in the products and services they deliver. At the same time, they must also create a sense of freedom. Doing this allows people to be their best selves, use their judgment to create extraordinary touchpoints, resolve unplanned issues that arise, and look for new ways of doing things in a better and faster way. And in order to avoid confusion, leaders need to be sure that their employees understand how framework and freedom differ and when to use each.

Let's break down each in more detail.

Framework

We have seen two forms of framework. The first is a framework that is driven *by purpose and values*. It includes a set of nonnegotiable and nonchanging beliefs, values, and even cultural practices for how to run and grow the organization. The second is a framework of *rules and policies* that must be followed exactly for regulatory, ethical, safety, process consistency, and quality reasons. This often represents a set of standards, such as cleanliness standards for a public restroom, a safety protocol for a hospital system, or standards and procedures for the safe preparation of food.

The Framework of Purpose and Values

The values-based framework often starts with purpose. The purpose-centered approach assumes that most of us are inspired to be part of something bigger than ourselves and make a difference in the world around us. For example, a home security company we worked with believes that its purpose of "keeping families safe" guides all interactions, while a toy retailer strives to "create the best 20 minutes of a child's day." Once purpose and values are clear, as they are in these two examples, most people don't need a script to bring the purpose and values to life in their everyday actions.

Organizations that use purpose and values as the framework for engaging the judgment and discretion of their people often use stories and examples as the means to help everyone in the organization understand what success looks like—stories and examples that describe what great healthcare, exceptional security for a family, or memorable retail experiences look like.

The Framework of Rules and Policies

A number of industries and organizations that require consistency of process for safety, security, and a differentiated customer experience to achieve predictable outcomes also have a framework that is driven by rules and policies. These industries include transportation, restaurant, hospitality, manufacturing, pharmaceutical, and entertainment.

One specific example of an organization in one of these industries is a Global 100 manufacturing company whose nonnegotiable policies are considered the "rules of the road." These rules are spelled out in detailed policies on everything from handling dangerous chemicals to who has the decision rights on investment decisions on the R&D required for new products. In our experience, it can be confusing to people to have both a framework *and* a freedom approach. It can be perceived as a conflict of directions, and people can feel paralyzed by not knowing where to start. One way to help people get unstuck is to help them see these apparent opposites coexisting on a continuum. We have found that people can make sense of this perceived conflict when we describe how they engage in terms of *hard lines*, *guidelines*, and *no lines*. Let's dive deeper into each:

- **Hard lines** are the areas where there is one organizational way of doing things—no exceptions. It is where a rule, a procedure, or a behavior is clearly defined, and we expect everyone in the organization to abide by it. There is no gray space.
- **Guidelines** come with "guardrails." Here boundaries are defined as firm, but how things get done between the guardrails is up to the individual. Guidelines are designed to be helpful and can be applied to areas like time and dollars or can be specific to an approach. With guidelines, you define expectations and provide guiding principles but leave the details of the "how" to the people executing it.
- **No lines** involves inviting people to use their special talents to do things as they see fit. No matter the situation, employees are free to solve problems in any way they deem appropriate— and are even encouraged to think outside the box.

The Framework and Freedom chart in Figure 4.3 provides more detail.

Freedom

Freedom invites individual creativity and discretionary effort. It trusts people to bring their best talents and skills to the opportunity to contribute to an organization or a winning team. Trust is based on the belief that once the context (the why and what) is defined, people have an amazing ability to respond with care, compassion, and creativity (the how) to deliver exceptional outcomes.

CONTROL	Spectrum of Control to Trust	TRUST
HARDLINES	**GUIDELINES**	**NO LINES**
VALUES BASED		
Example: Home Security Company	✔ Keep families safe	✔ Don't under serve or oversell security services	✔ Always consider and act as a guest in our customer's home
Hampton Hotels:	✔ Strengths - based approach ✔ **Purpose** - Fill the earth with the light and warmth of hospitality	✔ Language of Hamptonality ✔ DNA of **F**riendly, **A**uthentic, **C**aring, **T**houghtful (**F.A.C.T.**)	✔ **Sharecast** - Use strengths to bring FACT to life ✔ Create unique stories of FACT in action
RULES BASED		
Example: Airlines	✔ Pilot and mechanic safety process ✔ In-flight safety procedures	✔ Airplane boarding practices ✔ Service standards	✔ Passenger engage-ments of welcome, gratitude, and service
Restaurant:	✔ Key operating routines - Food safety process - Restaurant open and close process - Food preparation routines	✔ Customer is our north star ✔ People development and coaching ✔ Grow presence through community relationships	✔ Build relationships with customers ✔ Every touchpoint should create delight for customers
For Your People:	One Way ✔ ✔	Boundaries ✔ ✔	Incite Talent Skills ✔ ✔

root

FIGURE 4.3 *Framework and freedom*

Everyday Examples of Framework and Freedom

The easiest way to translate the paradox of framework and freedom into a complement of consistent standards and individual creativity is to provide an example of what it looks like when companies successfully combine the two. The goal is twofold—to see policies or processes strictly followed *and* to ask questions that invite individual thinking and creativity. A mindset with opposites makes the whole better. Just like a hot fudge sundae combines cold and hot, framework and freedom combine rigid "one way to do it" policies and processes with open invitations to add individual care, creativity, and judgment.

Let's look at a pair of practical examples where we see *framework*, which includes the "one way" of hard lines and the "firm boundaries" of guidelines, and *freedom*, which includes encouraging people to use their special talents as they see fit, combined and in action.

Example #1: The Hospital System

The framework-and-freedom approach at a hospital system includes strictly following protocol on quality and safety practices while at the same time inviting doctors, nurses, and staff to empathetically consider the perspective of the patient and patient's family.

Great patient experiences are highly dependent upon the quality of the personal interactions between providers and patients. Asking providers to show empathy, compassion, and respect creates the invitation to combine the complement of framework and freedom with the opportunity to elevate both patient and employee engagement. For example, there is a clear difference between a nurse just following quality standards (framework) and a nurse acting with empathy (freedom) in creating the patient's experience. In the first case, the nurse follows protocol exactly, answers questions when they are asked, and is polite in a routine way. It is, however, difficult to distinguish his or her communication from that of an automated help line where questions are anticipated and a canned answer is ready to be played back if you hit the right number. The engagement is polite and professional but clearly impersonal.

Now invite people to use their unique talents while also being empathetic, and you will see a nurse step into the whirlwind of anxious emotions that a patient and the patient's family are experiencing, while not losing the clinical point of view. Nurses with the freedom to bring their own empathy to the patient experience will find out how to speak a patient's language, compassionately question patients about their concerns or worries, and help connect the dots of information about their care. This type of nurse views understanding and responding to the perspective of the patient as an important part of the care experience.

Few stories tell this better than one told by Barry Schwartz in his book *Why We Work*. In an early chapter, Schwartz highlights a fascinating story told by researcher Amy Wrzesniewski about the way some people approach their work when invited to bring their special talents and are inspired by a meaningful purpose. The story is about Luke, a janitor in a teaching hospital. Luke explained why he cleaned the room of a comatose patient twice. Luke had cleaned this patient's room while the patient's father was outside smoking a cigarette. After the father returned from his break outside, he snapped and said he hadn't seen Luke clean the room. Luke explained, "At first, I got on the defensive and I was going to argue with him. But something caught me, and I said, 'I am sorry. I will go clean the room.' I cleaned it so that he could see me clean it. I could understand how he could be frustrated; it was like six months that his son was there. It was one of the few things he could do for his son. I could see how he would be a little frustrated, so I cleaned it again."

As researchers asked custodians to talk about their jobs at this hospital, they responded with stories about the fact that the official duties of cleaning were only a part of their job and that the other central part was to make patients and families feel comfortable, to divert them from their pain and fear, to promote health, and to relieve suffering. The framework and freedom for the janitors looked a lot like cleaning and comforting.

The formula in the healthcare example can apply to any organization or business. It's easy to see how when you break it down into clear hard lines, guidelines, and no lines. For example:

- **Hard lines.** Follow the "one-way" quality and safety protocols for patient treatment to ensure dispensing proper medication, avoiding infection, and facilitating healing.
- **Guidelines.** Establish firm boundaries such as a nurse can help explain processes but must refrain from interpreting tests or procedures.
- **No lines.** Be compassionate and empathetic with patients and their families and align with an overall mission to reduce suffering and enhance healing.

Now go back to the Framework and Freedom chart in Figure 4.3. For your own organization, describe the *hard lines* where you have nonnegotiable rules that need to be followed, the *guidelines* where firm boundaries exist, and *no lines* where you are inviting your people to step in and add their special talents and skills.

Example #2: The Hampton Way

Hampton by Hilton has been one of the most successful hotel brands of the past 30 years. The brand relies on franchising rather than company-owned hotels and is one of the most desired franchises to own in any industry. Hampton has been ranked by *Entrepreneur* magazine as the number one franchise on the Entrepreneur Franchise 500 list four times in five years. When owners are asked what makes Hampton so appealing, they frequently state: "You can sense the Hampton culture, which we call 'Hamptonality,' from property to property. It's not hard to create a culture when a company owns all its hotels. But when you have hundreds of franchisees and thousands of units, it's much harder. Hampton has done a phenomenal job of spreading that culture to all the owners in its brand."

One of the best examples of an organization combining the framework of shared standards with the freedom of individual creativity and discretion is described by Gina Valenti, former vice president of brand hospitality at Hilton. The way she tells it, "The uniqueness that our people bring to a Hampton is what sets us apart, and we must create freedom in our culture to invite that uniqueness to be part of the guest experience every day."

She further states, "Processes like Six Sigma and Lean work to eliminate variability, but this approach doesn't work when looking to create unique experiences because we eliminate the individualized touch that only human beings can provide when they have some freedom to be their best selves."

In Valenti's many years of working with the Hampton brand, she has experienced a lot of change in culture. Traditionally, the company took a very guarded approach to talking about people because Hampton is a franchised organization and people are employed by the owners and operators. So originally there was a lot of scripting, prescribing, and traditional training.

Valenti explains:

> The real game-changer for us happened in 2004.
> The brand launched something we called "Make it
> Hampton," which represented the launch of 127 product
> changes and innovations. By 2005, the initiative was so
> successful that all of our competitors started copying
> many aspects of it, thereby eroding the competitive
> advantage we received from those product introduc-
> tions pretty quickly. Our team got together and had
> an "aha" moment. We couldn't just keep evolving the
> product because we would evolve ourselves out of the
> category and the pocketbook of our owners and guests.
> So, our focus shifted to the uniqueness of people and
> team member engagement as a differentiator.

Because of that, the question became, "How do we unleash the uniqueness of people in the best way without creating chaos in the system?" Hampton still had firm standards for many things in a hotel. There were standards for owners, for amenities, and for products that a hotel had to carry. There were hard lines for staff in relation to food safety, cleanliness of rooms, and maintenance. But when it came to culture, Hampton moved exclusively to a combination of guidelines and no lines.

The question for Hampton was, "How do we unlock that wonderful potential that we believe sits within just about every human being?" The answer started to unfold when Hampton crossed paths with author and speaker Marcus Buckingham, who focuses on building strength-based organizations.

"We started by becoming a strengths-based organization and started engaging our general managers in how to identify their strengths and how to lead strengths-based teams. But strengths were only the beginning of sustainably differentiating the brand from the competition and creating unique experiences for guests," Valenti says.

Hampton created a "Brand Compass," which is essentially its purpose. The goal was to have the Brand Compass be easy to understand, relatable, and actionable for all team members around the globe. Hampton defined its Brand Compass by explaining, "We focus on the little things that make a big difference to create memorable experiences worth sharing."

Hampton is very deliberate when it comes to language. The company believes that language matters and connects the Hampton network worldwide. In the words of Valenti, "Language puts a name to what we know, what we feel. It links us together and creates a vernacular that aligns us."

The culture movement that had started to form was called "Hamptonality" and was inspired by a Lloyd Price song called "Personality." The original song lyrics—"Cause you've got personality"—were changed to "We've got Hamptonality," and team members filmed a video at a hotel that showed all of them singing along. It did a wonderful job capturing the essence of the personality of Hampton and its team members. Before you knew it, many hotels started creating their own versions of the video and posting them on YouTube. You will still find many of them if you go to YouTube and search "Hamptonality."

The goal of this original video was to capture that Hamptonality spirit in the proverbial bottle and find ways to scale it better. Valenti's team went around the world and asked hotel team members what Hamptonality meant to them, because Valenti and her team didn't want to script it or to come up with a corporate definition. The belief in what the brand stood for and the secrets to Hamptonality already existed because it was in the organizations' DNA. The leaders had trust and belief in their people (freedom), so the leadership just needed to curate, codify, and nurture it.

Around the world, people excitedly explained what the word Hamptonality meant to them. They drew pictures, symbols, and words. Almost immediately, common themes and images rose to the top. Happy faces, winks, and smiles became *friendly*. Many of the stick figures people drew shared a sense of being *authentic*. The many hearts that were drawn became *caring*. And the stories about the small but meaningful things that team members would do for guests became *thoughtful*. As a result, Hampton unleashed a powerful DNA, or set of values: Friendly, Authentic, Caring, and Thoughtful (FACT).

"We didn't hire a consultant or an agency to come up with what Hamptonality should mean for our people and then roll out a prescribed way on how all our people should act," Valenti says. "What we did do was create powerful guidelines for people to express themselves in a way that is consistent with the brand, but unique to them."

Valenti adds, "Once we had our Brand Compass, strengths, the language, and spirit of Hamptonality, and the DNA of Friendly,

Authentic, Caring, and Thoughtful (FACT), we had a framework to help inspire team members to see what they could do to bring to life Hilton's broader purpose, which is to 'fill the earth with the light and warmth of hospitality.'"

But that is not all that was required to create industry-leading performance for owners and guests.

Hampton has created online and offline training courses on the FACT DNA and how to bring it to life with guests. The organization created a best-practice sharing site called Sharecast where hotel managers and team members could ask questions and share ideas. This online digital tool for Hampton team members already has thousands of voluntary users and tens of thousands of comments with ideas, and the site continues to grow. And because Hampton trusted the hotels to use it wisely, the site is not moderated or monitored.

Hampton also created "FACT Packs," which are giftlike packages that are sent to all 2,000+ hotels several times a year to connect them in a productive and engaging way. One month, the box might focus on how to engage kids at the hotel during the summer, the next might be focused on how every team member can help build the brand of the hotel and sell in the local community, while another might be on supporting a good cause during a global month of service.

The point is that there were many deliberate and planned interactions that helped the organization. All of its work has led team members to want to inspire and coach others on how to be the best version of themselves, lead with Hamptonality, and contribute, no matter where they are in the organization.

When asked what is most difficult about this approach, Phil Cordell, the global brand leader for Hampton for over 20 years, said:

> It is being comfortable with some things you can't control and that some stuff will get created in the field that

you are not proud of. But the reality is that for every one of those, you will get 20 that are way better than anything you could have ever thought of. Plus, it has an energy and a momentum that you could never create in a corporate boardroom or in a training department.

So, in short, create an ecosystem that people can work within, one in which people constantly inspire others and reinforce new expressions of the movement you are looking to create. Then get out of the way and let your people play to their strengths to create differentiating experiences that can't be duplicated.

In Valenti's words, "Who are we to prescribe a script for them to follow when they are working in the real world of helping guests and serving guests each day?"

GET YOUR PEOPLE TO INVEST IN YOU

The greatest way to inspire employees to deliver exceptional performances is to make them truly invested in the organization. People must believe it's *their* store, *their* hotel, *their* office, *their* factory, or *their* hospital. They must feel that they're more than a cog in a wheel with overseers watching and waiting to catch them in a screwup.

We can't tap deep discretionary effort if we hold people to just rules and procedures. We want them to do more than "play not to lose." We want them to "play to win," which requires stepping away from the company playbook in certain circumstances and adding what is unique about them to make things better. We can tap real discretionary effort only when we ask people for their judgment and creativity, when we invite them to participate and consider what they bring to the table, when we use words like "buy-in," "advocacy," and "ownership." But those words mean nothing if we don't invite people to be part of it. The only way to succeed in earning an employee's discretionary effort is to get the employee involved and "bought in."

Typically, the widespread approach has been to tell people to "do it this way, and we'll hold you accountable." Clearly, this is defining and *limiting*. Compare this with defining and *freeing*. It's difficult for leaders to take this step, as you must protect your customers and your reputation. But when people are tied to policy, it's "just a job." The better way is to inspire people to believe that what they're doing is a passionate pursuit of a larger goal.

HOW YOUR EMPLOYEES SHAPE YOUR REPUTATION

There's no question that consumer expectations are very different from what they were just a few years ago. Once, people largely expected reliability and consistency. When you traveled, you simply required a clean hotel and a decent restaurant. If you weren't satisfied, you just didn't return, and you might have told a few friends about your experience. Not that long ago, advertising controlled information flow to consumers. We learned about products and services and how good or bad they were from magazines, TV, or comments made by friends and family.

To say this has changed is a monumental understatement.

Today individual businesses no longer control the narrative. The new era of transparency has forever transformed things. The way in which your front-line employees express the spirit of your company—what you're trying to bring to life—deeply affects your image in the marketplace.

Any mishap or incident can now find a worldwide platform through personal networks or sites like TripAdvisor. If something bad happens, there's a good chance that someone will post a picture or share the story in a place where possibly millions of people will see it. Those experiences are now shaping public perception about the type of company you are. Your employees' behaviors make an enormous difference in your reputation today.

Here's an example. Say you're traveling in a new city, and you want coffee. You check Yelp and see that there's a Dunkin' Donuts nearby. It has two stars. Then you find a local place with *four* stars. You're more likely to go there. Regardless of how many Dunkin' Donuts commercials you have seen, you are more likely to rely on what customers themselves have said, and it's likely shaped by great experiences provided by local employees. A big brand gives you a head start, but in the social media age, you must earn your business one store, one location, and one experience at a time. It's essentially trench warfare for your customer, with social media being the great equalizer for the little guy. Social media has redefined the rules of the game. This is one of the key reasons why companies need to look deeply into this flawed belief—that employees are just there to follow rules.

So what *do* customers want now? In this era of transparency, they want unique, authentic, and personalized experiences such as boutique hotels and locally grown foods. What they *don't* want is to be exposed to scripted experiences by a company.

ADDRESSING THE BLIND SPOT CHANGES THE RESULT

Operating on the flawed belief that human variability needs to be minimized to create scalability and consistency is clearly failing companies. Successful companies are rejecting the idea of creating systems that require people—indeed, *motivate* them—to contribute at the lowest common denominator of their defined activities. Amazing things can happen when companies trust their people to use their reasonable judgment to serve a customer and make a lasting impression.

True story: A couple of years ago, we flew to Connecticut to visit a new client. We picked up our rental car and drove to our hotel, which was about a 20-minute drive from our client's offices.

This was a new relationship, and we wanted to make a good first impression. Our meeting was at 8 a.m. the next day, so we agreed to meet at 7:25 a.m. sharp.

On that cold and rainy morning, we were in the car right on time. One of our consultants traveling with us turned the key in the ignition. Nothing happened. He tried again. Nada. You probably know that miserable, sinking feeling we had. But we needed a plan B, and fast. We rushed into the hotel lobby and beseeched the general manager. Taxi? None available right now, and it was pre-Uber. Hotel shuttle? Out, with no expected time of return. The sinking feeling got a few feet deeper.

As we started to dial our client's number to tell her that we'd be seriously late, the general manager asked us to wait and picked up the phone to call the competitor across the street. We stood in awe as she arranged for *the competitor's* shuttle to take us to our meeting. She smiled. We smiled! Not only did we get a ride to our client meeting, but the hotel staff made sure we had fresh coffee to calm us down on our ride. The staff waved goodbye to us as we rode away.

Would the world have ended if we'd been late? No. But anyone in business knows that there are important moments where showing up on time makes a significant difference. And really, the point here isn't that we made the meeting. It's that the general manager's actions weren't in any training script. She surely wasn't following hotel protocol. In fact, it probably violated property and hotel rules to get us the competitor's shuttle.

But it was the *exact right thing to do*, and any hotel owner and franchisee would be extremely proud of how those team members responded to us. Their actions created tremendous customer loyalty. This is what can happen when a company allows an employee to use her own judgment, get creative, and do the appropriate thing for a customer. And yes, it was a Hampton.

Now here's a question: Has this ever happened to you? How many hotel staffs would have acted that way and been truly "in it" with you to that degree? Nowhere in any manual on how to be a good hotel general manager does it say, "Call a competitor." The most common response would be to call an outside service provider—a reasonable effort. But that's not what this situation called for.

The general manager even told us that she felt she had the freedom to do this for us. She had a goal: solve the problem for us. This is what "freedom in the framework" looks like. It's feeling empowered and knowing that your leaders (when they find out) will *celebrate* you rather than punish you.

We think Valenti said it well when she suggested, "The freedom and uniqueness that our people bring to our organization every day is what sets us apart and is the true source of our competitive differentiation." It is the job of the leader to invite that uniqueness to be part of the work experience every day. However, the key to doing this well is helping people embrace the paradox of hard lines and no lines at the same time. Generally, when people hear these seemingly inconsistent ideas, they are confused. The key is to help people understand that we need to eliminate human variability on the "hard lines" to be consistent, and to add human variability where there are "no lines" to add the individual care and judgment that create better results.

CHAPTER FIVE

Leadership Blind Spot #5: **TRUTH**

Common Misconception

My people feel safe telling me what they really think and feel.

The Basics

In many leadership teams, what people really think often gets discussed in the hallways and bathrooms and by the watercooler rather than in meeting rooms. People don't feel safe telling the truth because they don't think it is smart or safe to do so. Many leaders believe that to be effective and successful, they need to be smarter than the next guy, fight for their area of the business, and not show vulnerability. This mentality creates lack of trust, collaboration, and common ownership for a greater goal—and ultimately greatly slows down execution speed.

The Question We Will Answer

What can we do as leaders to make it safe for our people to tell the truth and act on those truths to make the business better?

From an early age, we're told to tell the truth. In most cases, that served us well. Now think of your own early career experiences. How often did you dare to speak the "real truth" to your leaders? Most people answer, "Hardly ever." So why is it that when we are the leaders, we forget this? Or better yet, how can we get rid of the flawed belief that "people feel safe telling me what they really think and feel."

According to recent data, the trend of not being candid with higher-ups is getting worse rather than better. The recent Edelman Trust Barometer shows that people's trust of their CEO and CEOs in general is at an all-time low. Sixty-three percent of survey respondents said CEOs are somewhat or not at all credible. That is 12 points lower than the previous year's results!

Truth telling is not a core competency for today's organizations, and leaders, consciously or subconsciously, have not created an environment where truth telling is safe, appreciated, or rewarded.[1]

The costs of not having a culture where it is safe to tell the truth are significant. It could be information not reaching the boss because no one wants to pass on the bad news. It could be departments not sharing information because it might put them in a bad light with peers. It could even be that the hassle and perceived consequences of telling the truth are not worth the cost for people in the company.

On a daily basis, friction like this kills speed, collaboration, and quality decision making. And if truth telling is hard on a day-to-day basis, imagine how much harder it must be to tell the truth in the midst of a crisis.

If you still think it is safe for your people to say what they truly think and feel, consider these two real-life examples:

1. A pilot was busy figuring out why his plane was experiencing trouble. As he was feverishly diagnosing the mechanics, his copilot kept some critical information from him because he didn't want to disturb the pilot. That information was that the plane's fuel was dangerously low—and in the end, the plane crashed.

2. A patient was waiting for a relative's kidney to arrive so he could have a lifesaving transplant. Some deliveries got mixed up, and even though a nurse noticed the problem, she didn't speak up. As a result, someone else mistakenly disposed of the kidney, and the operation was canceled.

In both cases, someone didn't speak up, likely because the person didn't feel he or she was "allowed" to do so as a result of sanctioned habits, established hierarchies, and toxic cultures. Many people feel it's simply not safe to speak up to a superior when something is clearly amiss. And this doesn't even consider the great ideas that people keep to themselves about innovation and a better path to higher performance. Unless you as a leader very consciously create approaches and mechanisms for truth telling, the truth will often not be spoken.

ESTABLISHING A CULTURE OF TRUTH

A culture of truth telling requires leaders to be vulnerable and to create a place where people feel safe telling the truth.

We had the opportunity to work with a global financial services firm for a leadership development assignment. Our charge was to help with a leadership offsite for the top 100. One of the goals was to get better at having open and honest conversations. We find that skills are often best practiced with real and relevant content, so we decided to practice having honest conversations using the topic of the current state of the business.

We conducted confidential interviews with a subset of people in the top 100 to get their perspective on the strategy, the state of the leadership team, and opportunity areas for the business. The organization was a successful one, but some of the feedback mentioned that there was a significant hierarchy and that people were not necessarily comfortable challenging their superiors. There were also some questions about how the company's strategy and initiatives connected to one another.

One way we often bring out challenging issues is by drawing some of these realities in an exaggerated way and adding humor to it, as this depersonalizes issues and makes it safer to speak honestly. Think of it like a customized *Dilbert* cartoon.

We broke the top 100 into groups of 8 and engaged them in a dialogue using the cartoonlike sketch and a set of questions to guide the conversation. We were roaming the room to make sure things were working, and about 15 minutes in, people were giving us nods and thumbs up. One person came over and told us that she and the other members of her group had never had dialogue this honest and open at the firm. There was positive buzz in the room, and everyone seemed excited about the way issues of conflict, adversity, and overall frustration were openly discussed. We overheard explicit comments about this being a new day and a new way for leaders to have difficult conversations more comfortably, and that these conversations could help address the main roadblocks of the business. We were sitting on a breakthrough moment, and you could feel it. The session was designed to be about 50 minutes, and after about 35 minutes, we noticed the head of strategy walk toward the CEO, who had just entered the room.

Our sketch raised some unresolved issues on the strategy of the company, and the honest conversations people were having brought those issues to the forefront. In hindsight, we should have explained our process to the head of strategy a bit better than we had done, but addressing that now would not help the situation. Because the CEO had joined the room later than everyone else, he missed out on the positive buzz that was felt by everyone else in the room. So as his head of strategy filled him in on what he had missed, the CEO began to feel that the conversation was an attack on his strategy.

Prior to this point, we had not had the opportunity to build a relationship with the CEO, so we knew we were in a bit of trouble.

A couple of days later, we heard from the CEO, and he cut right to the chase. He opened the meeting with: "That was quite the set of conversations we had at our leadership session. I am not sure how you got to that content. We went back to everyone you interviewed, and they told us that the picture you painted for us does not reflect the content they shared with you."

We knew the account was on the line with the answer we would give, but we also knew that if we could not make a meaningful connection here, this would not be a productive relationship for either side. So it was time to lay it all on the line.

We dove right in and said, "We appreciate the honest feedback, and ultimately this leaves you with two alternatives. The first is that we have a vivid imagination and are great exaggerators of reality. The second is that many of your people are not comfortable telling you the truth, and as a result, a lot of valuable information is kept from you and the executive team. So if you want to have more open and honest conversations, your people need to feel safer. And that type of environment is nowhere close to where you are right now or where you need it to be. If you believe the first alternative is realistic, you should just fire us. If you believe there is truth to the second, we can really help."

It was quiet for about five seconds, and then he gave us a nod and a smile. He told us he appreciated our courage. He explained that he wanted a culture with more trust and was curious about the role he could play to help that. We have worked with him and his leadership team for several years and since created a stronger culture of transparency, truth telling, and elevated performance.

Truth telling is hard, and as Figure 5.1 highlights, unless leaders foster an environment where it is constantly nurtured and reinforced, bad habits prevail.

FIGURE 5.1   *Truth-telling is hard.*

Of course, truth is not absolute. What people see, perceive, or feel can be completely off-base or accurately spot-on. Either way, you want those facts, perceptions, or feelings to be openly processed within an organization. The open processing lets you work with the relevant truths and debunk what isn't accurate but likely creates organizational distraction. If people feel like the truth gets scrutinized the way your electronics are at airport security, you have an issue. And in most organizations, unfortunately, that is the case.

Over the past 20 years we have seen what can happen when people are invited and encouraged to share what they see and feel as the truth. At first, they are resistant and reserved when it comes to saying what they think and feel about organizational performance, company culture, and team dynamics. However, when they feel that it's safe to share the truth and that they're valued for revealing it, it's as if they are truly reinvigorated. They feel that their perspective is valued, and they experience a sense of new hope because they can finally talk about the real issues that hold them back. They are also excited about the possibility that the values of the organization and their personal values might come closer together than they ever thought possible.

We can't overstate the impact truth telling can have on the engagement, optimism, and hope people feel about their organization and their team. Truth telling makes all the difference if you want your teams to successfully work together.

THE MYSTIQUE OF THE SHARED ARMREST

It's strange but true that we'll often be more honest with a total stranger than with people we've worked with for years. When we're stuck in an airline seat where we have to share an armrest, anonymity takes over. With the person beside you, you don't just share the armrest, but you get the same pretzels, the same plastic cup of water, the same leg space, and the same turbulence. You're equals suffering through the same experience—at least for the duration of the flight. This shared experience breaks down barriers, gives us a sense of connection, and allows us to share our stories, feelings, and concerns more openly. When it comes to talking to a total stranger, we speak with candor and intimacy in a way that's natural and authentic. Conversations flow effortlessly, human to human.

What stops us from talking with the same candor and vulnerability with people we've worked with for years? Why is it so hard for leaders to foster an environment that has people comfortable telling the truth? And why does it seem so hard to do at work, while in other instances it happens naturally? The truth is that it's very rare to find an organization where people are routinely truthful. And the higher you go in an organization, the rarer truth telling becomes. This is the norm because the only safe havens are behind closed doors. As truth telling declines, cost, bureaucracy, redundancies, and lack of confidence in the future all rise. The practice of effectively telling the truth may be the single most significant catalyst in creating positive and meaningful change. It may also be the biggest ingredient in making people feel safe so they can bring the best version of themselves to the workplace.

And both inability and fear are present for all sides—when employees talk to leaders and when leaders have to face the truth.

THE POWER DIFFERENTIAL

If we know honesty plays a large part in company success, why don't we tell each other the truth? Why do so many fiercely protect *what is* instead of building *what could be*? Why are we more inclined to tell others what we think they want to hear instead of what we truly think and feel?

The answers are complex, but let's start with the issue of power. There are really two kinds of power: authentic and inauthentic. The foundations for authentic power and leadership are compassion, vulnerability, and empathy.

Inauthentic power is all about status, rank, possessions, and authority. With inauthentic power, it's the mindset that:

- I *have* more than you do.
- I *know* more than you do.
- I *am* more than you are.

Inauthentic power, spurred on by our egos, makes it hard for us to understand what others are feeling. It also makes it especially hard for us to tell each other the truth about how we think and feel—and really *hear* it. This is difficult because truth telling isn't a core competency of most companies, teams, or leaders.

There's actually a scientific explanation for the power issue. Researchers tell us that when authority and power go to your head, it turns off your heart.[2] Power diminishes empathy in the brain. Power changes how the brain operates in fundamental ways and makes it hard to feel and understand what other people feel and understand. And there's a kicker—the more powerful you become, the harder it is to remain an authentic leader. But it's not just the CEO who is impacted by this "power disease" that robs us of authenticity; everyone within a company can be affected. Because of how the brain works, humans lose empathy when they get a few more direct reports, a promotion, a raise, or a better office. They say power corrupts, but it also separates us from the connections that make us human.

UNDERSTANDING FEAR

Fear is the ultimate truth killer. Unfortunately, most company cultures have some level of fear that holds people back from truthful and transparent conversations that are found in high-performing organizations. Fear slows everything down. It causes hesitation, induces stress, and keeps thousands of people from contributing what they are capable of at work.

In an interview with the *Harvard Business Review,* James Detert, a professor at Cornell's Johnson Graduate School of Management, said that it is natural to keep your guard up in the workplace. In his words, "We have a deep set of defense mechanisms that make us careful around people in authority positions." The common reality is that people in all levels of organizations are silenced by fear.[3]

Why Employees Are Afraid to Tell the Truth at Work

There are eight common fears that hold people back from truth telling, and they all perpetuate limiting beliefs. These fears can appear singly or in combination.

1.   The fear of indictment for past performance
     Questions asked: Is it safe to ask about this? Will it make me look stupid for an action or decision I made in the past?

2.   The fear of being branded and punished for not being on board
Questions asked: If I speak up and disagree, will I be the team member who doesn't get to play? Should I go along just because it's easier?

3.   The fear of offending a teammate or colleague
Question asked: We have a great relationship, but can I be sure you'll take my comments in the right way, even if it's for the good of the business?

4.   The fear of losing status on the team
Questions asked: Should I jeopardize my place in the group? Should I risk losing my sense of importance and influence?

5.   The fear that speaking the truth will sap valuable time and energy, and issues will never be resolved anyway
Questions asked: Should I open a can of worms? Do I want to be the one who brings up the unsolvable, who talks about what's wrong?

6.   The fear that what I have to say may not be that good
Questions asked: If I talk about things from my perspective, will people think less of me because of my answers? And even if I do speak up, will they value my opinions?

7.   The fear that my leader really doesn't want to hear bad news
Questions asked: If I say what I think, could that be a career-limiting move? Is this really the smart thing for me to do?

8.   The fear of letting people know you really don't have it all figured out
Questions asked: What if I say something that proves I don't have the answers? Should I risk looking like a beginner on this topic or issue?

One way to encourage truth telling is to acknowledge the eight fears that people often feel. Get the fears out in the open by name and ask for a show of hands by people who can identify with them. In many ways, conveying to people what their fears might be, or what common fears might look like before people experience them, suggests that as leaders we know what it is like to be them and that we want to make it safer and easier to speak up.

Why Leaders Are Afraid to Hear the Truth

Centuries ago, every king and queen had someone who would always tell them the unvarnished truth in a way that they could easily accept and understand. This person would also point out errors and misjudgments without fearing that he'd be fired. This person, called the court jester, was expected to tell the king or queen unpleasant news that no one else would dare talk about—even to point out the ruler's personal shortcomings. Just imagine how valuable a jester could be in business organizations! This person could show others the hard truth in a simple way without fear of punishment (and get paid to do so).

The reason court jesters were so effective is because truth telling can require removing leader blinders. Often, those closest to the truth can't hear or see what is right in front of them. Additionally, it is very difficult for anyone to speak truth to power, as the fear of negative repercussions is often present.

Another way to look at this is to recognize that—just like employees in an organization—leaders have fears that get in the way of truth-telling cultures and practices. Exposing these fears can be as helpful to a leader as it is to employees when it comes to recognizing and reducing the fears that inhibit truth telling.

Let's examine the core drivers of why leaders often don't create an environment of truth telling:

1. No leader wants to have people revolting in the kingdom, and the leader may feel that any criticism could take on a life of its own.

    Questions asked: Is this an indictment of my leadership? Am I doing something wrong? Are others coming after me?

2. Most leaders find it hard to see how a "bitch session" of critique, criticism, and dissatisfaction can turn into a powerful force for positive change.

    Questions asked: How can complaining move us forward? Isn't this a grand waste of time? Why are all these people whining instead of proposing ways to make it better? Aren't they just venting?

3. Leaders don't want to invite people to play the "monkey game."

    Questions asked: If we talk about what's really happening, won't they expect me to solve their problems? If I open the door to truth telling, won't they all just dump their "monkeys" on my desk?

4. Leaders don't want to admit they don't have all the answers—even more so than employees who feel this way.

    Questions asked: Will people stop believing I'm a quality leader if I admit I don't know everything? Will I lose their respect?

5. Leaders do not know how to have candid truth conversations and have it match their picture of what leaders do.

    Questions asked: How do I allow complaining and still be a strong leader, especially when the complaining usually includes finger-pointing and comes with a lack of accountability from the people I am responsible for leading?

Few things are more important to improving a leader's readiness to hear the truth than making their own fears part of their own considerations for crafting an environment where everyone is open to telling and hearing the truth. Leaders often ooze confidence. It is an important attribute of good leaders. However, an even more important trait for leaders who want to make truth telling a priority is getting comfortable with public vulnerability and seeing it as a sign of strong leadership. Being able to admit and share times of weakness and uncertainty and obvious examples of where you could have done a better job in a public setting is a way to earn trust from those you lead. Psychologist Tasha Eurich says the "higher someone is on the corporate ladder, the harder it is to be self-aware, including the harder it is for a leader to want to admit their weaknesses and vulnerabilities." She calls this the "CEO disease."[4]

Once you have an environment at the top where it does not feel safe to tell the truth, it tends to permeate throughout the entire organization. There is a big price to pay when leaders falsely believe that their people are sharing all the truths they need to hear to run a successful business.

WHEN LEADERS REFUSE TO FACE THE TRUTH

A lack of truth telling among members of a leadership team can have profound effects. When team members do not engage in the right conversations, even when spending an entire day together, they fail to address the real issues holding them back, as the following example shows.

A large retail client that we worked with had thousands of stores and a big problem—the corporate office had stopped listening to store managers because they were complaining a lot and it was "impossible to make them happy." Managers had stopped telling corporate what they thought because "they weren't listening anyhow." Both sides blamed "the other guy" for blocking company success, and the relationship between corporate and the field was steadily deteriorating. Company leaders realized that things were not heading in the right direction and wanted to work with us to change the trajectory of what was happening.

We did ethnographic research within the business by observing what was going on, rather than just interviewing or surveying people within the organization. This is often one of the best ways to get at the truth and serves things up in a way that is difficult to refute. In the end, we discovered that no one was listening to the other side, and other core issues needed to come to light.

At the corporate level, the executives had a mixed set of ideas on what they wanted the stores to do, and there was something amounting to a "civil war" between new executive talent with innovative ideas and old talent who felt the current direction was the right way to go. As a result, the field was getting mixed messages. This conflict also led the decision making and responsiveness at the leadership level to significantly slow down.

As we spent time in the field, we also learned that people were committed to their products and services, but they were paying more attention to *those* things instead of their customers. So they had gotten efficient at putting up displays at the right time, restocking items effectively, and running core operations well, but they were so focused operationally that they were not great at making meaningful connections with their customers. They had clean stores with the right inventory, but they were not connecting authentically with their customers the way the competition was. And they didn't see this customer disconnect in the field, but they were seeing the absence of being customer centric at corporate, as the customer satisfaction surveys were making that truth obvious.

Trust and communication had broken down within leadership and across the business, and the result was a culture of apathy and nonperformance. Not only was this not safe or smart, but no one took the time or even cared to listen.

The leaders started to address this dysfunctional reality with several actions. As corporate leaders, they decided to leave their egos in their offices and visited stores with a true curiosity about what it was like to work in one of several thousand retail stores. They quickly found out that corporate kept sending dozens of contradictory messages on a weekly basis that made it impossible to both follow orders and be successful. They even drew a picture of what it felt like to be a store general manager, and the picture showed a manager at the end of an initiatives pipe that had hundreds of requests bombarding him (Figure 5.2).

FIGURE 5.2 *Manager initiative overload*

The change that was instituted was that everything had to be aligned and simplified at the corporate level before it went to the field, and corporate began to see the stores as partners that had to be set up for success instead of an outlet that had to be pushed hard to generate the required sales. The stores began to see corporate as more of a servant leader that was acting to remove the burdens that were in the way of their success at the store level. The first step toward success was getting the truth from the store manager and acting on it.

MAKING IT SAFE FOR OUR PEOPLE TO TELL THE TRUTH—HUMOR IN PICTURES

As human beings with fears, we don't automatically perform at our full potential; we perform at our belief level. Fear and anxiety often conspire to drive those beliefs to lower levels. In most companies, the powerful and powerless are hopelessly out of touch with each other. Employees fear talking about the truth in meetings or even at their workstations. In fact, at work, most of us tell each other the truth in just three places—in the bathroom, in the hallway, and at the watercooler.

The antidote lies in getting comfortable with public vulnerability. It's about keeping the blinders off so you create a culture that makes it safe and smart to tell the truth.

To face the truth with success (and the least amount of pain) is to address it with a sense of humor and visualization. Case in point: *Dilbert* cartoons. Scott Adams's visual stories are so successful because they make it safe to laugh at situations that we can't always talk about. They make light of things that ring true almost everywhere, and they can tee up collective chuckles that have the potential to lead to powerful conversations about things that we all know are true but don't know how to talk about without upsetting other people.

Because change is an emotional process and we want to change our environment to one that encourages truth telling, we need to find ways to make this possible. And a humorous visual can be a powerful tool for starting and sustaining tough conversations that move us toward that environment. Like a good *Saturday Night Live* skit, humor invites us to enjoy candor and realism. The essence of the good laugh is often in its truth!

In our experience, we find that cartoons of the situations or "truths we are frustrated with" create astounding breakthrough conversations for three reasons:

1. Visualizing or making the hidden whispers of the workplace tangible immediately sends a message that we sanction this conversation. It shouts, "It's safe to discuss the undiscussables!"
2. Cartoons visualize what many people think and feel and bring instant credibility to their perspective. It is a form of emotional intelligence that makes talking about the so-called elephants in the room a great deal easier.
3. Cartoons don't define which images are the "most true." Instead this is up to teams and leaders to decide. And as they do, the shared vulnerability and peer accountability that emerge are unique and many times game changing.

MEET ME AT THE WATERCOOLER

For more than 15 years, we have duplicated the "watercooler experience" and watched the truth emerge. So what is a watercooler experience? As we said above, in most organizations candid conversations only occur in three places: in the bathroom, in the hallway, and at the watercooler. The "watercooler" can be the actual office watercooler, or it might be the coffee dispenser or the kitchen refrigerator. Wherever it is, candid comments are exchanged with ease here.

The watercooler experience makes it as easy to speak with the same truth and candor in official meetings as people feel in the informal, "safe" places (in the bathroom and hallway and at the watercooler). The watercooler concept involves essentially two main steps: (1) assessing what people on a team or in an organization feel are the current realities that are most responsible for holding them back and that they are frustrated with and (2) depicting these issues using cartoons or humorous sketches—which we call Watercooler® visuals— on a tabletop-sized paper so that they can be openly discussed by a team or multiple teams.

We've watched transformations happen in real time in places as diverse as boardrooms of $50 billion companies and shop floors of factories. We've found that humorous sketches are the absolute best way to safely support the critical conversations that most people don't know how to have. A conversation around a sketch fosters an environment where people can overcome their fears, be vulnerable, and explore the truths that creatively dissatisfy them. They create a haven that frees truth telling to capture relevance, humor, vulnerability, and shared accountability. By visualizing the truth in humorous sketches that tightly focus on the issues that need to be discussed, we can draw people immediately and safely into difficult conversations.

This is because when people "see their feelings" in a picture, it's hard to look away. It's a validation that how they feel is OK. Compare this with being given facts and figures or being talked at and told about the urgency to change. In a sketch that captures how people feel, all defenses go down.

The good news is that even powerful leaders can be coached into returning to their compassionate and authentic selves, to create a sense of shared public vulnerability—a "level relating field."

THE ART OF GETTING PEOPLE TO TELL THE TRUTH

Authentic conversations are hard—and rare. Structures and hierarchies have a tremendous impact on the ability to have honest conversations. Art offers a way to overcome this situation.

For example, one organization that we were working with had a senior team that was struggling to lead the company during challenging economic times. The team members individually felt like the team was underperforming in leading the company, and for sure these leaders felt they were falling short as role models for the hundreds of other senior leaders in the organization. They just didn't know how to go about changing it. Interestingly, each member of the team had a good handle on the root causes behind the dysfunction of the team, but the members were reluctant to bring these issues up. To make matters worse, half the team was brand-new and the other half had been there over 20 years, so a rift between the seasoned leaders (old guard) and the new leaders (new guard) became a real roadblock.

After we reviewed the interview findings, we skipped summarizing the results in a PowerPoint deck with an executive summary and frequency rankings. Instead we decided to draw a picture of the truths that they were telling us but were not comfortable telling each other. The picture of that Watercooler® sketch is shown in Figure 5.3.

The sketch focused on a set of humorous depictions of the truth—the behaviors of this senior team were, at times, childlike at best, and in some cases spoiled-childlike. For example, these were some of the major issues that surfaced and demanded that the team talk about:

1. The dominant overall theme of executives playing in their individual executive sandboxes building their individual castles rather than all executives working together to build one castle became the main theme of the sketch. "Not playing nice in the sandbox" took on a whole new meaning for the senior leaders as it stung a bit, but it was undeniably the truth—as told to us by almost each one of the executives.

FIGURE 5.3 *The leadership sandbox*

2. Not only did the old guard–new guard chasm separate individual executives based on tenure, but the chasm was growing wider by the day and threatened to infect the culture of the organization.

3. Up in the left corner of the sketch, the decision board with the "decision Post-it Notes" falling off captured the fact that as a team, the executives made decisions but rarely stuck with any of them. At times, the leaders couldn't even tell if they had made a decision on some of the most pressing issues facing the business.

4. Last, on the right side of the sketch, you can see a leader, like a child, burying the real issues in the sand, or in the case of this team, burying the critical business issues that carried any conflict and adversity. In this case, they didn't use sand, but they found a way to make the issues unclear or ambiguous.

Once these issues saw the light of day and the members of the team found a way to discuss which ones were most true and which ones were less true, they cracked the code of silence around the real issues holding them back. The team accomplished more in the next three months than it did in the previous year in addressing and improving the most important issues for the company.

DRAWING OUT THE TRUTH

Drawings that reveal a deeper truth can be powerful conversation starters. Below are three vignettes that we have used with clients to serve up difficult conversations that teams did not know how to have. These vignettes—about leadership dynamics and behaviors that need to be addressed—could be worth showing in a meeting to trigger a conversation if your organization is dealing with a similar issue.

Example 1: Lazy Culture Sketch

FIGURE 5.4 *Lazy culture*

The cartoon sketch in Figure 5.4 was for a glass manufacturing company that had a culture where business as usual was acceptable. Many people expressed it as a "comfort culture" privately but never took a strong stand publicly. The sketch of the glass in a reclining chair, without ambition, sparked an intense conversation over whether the imagery was true or not, about what sustained this "make the product and see if it sells" approach, and even about why talent that is at best below average was not dealt with throughout the organization.

That day, the meeting participants decided that they couldn't look at the lazy culture cartoon and not do something drastic about it. It collectively hit home, and as a result, the team decided that action needed to be taken. The company accelerated its transformation to a consumer products company, and the leadership team began to build a successful change movement to create a culture that could enable that transformation—something the company had not been able to do up to that point.

Example 2: Leaders Rappelling into the Weeds

The sketch in Figure 5.5 was for a Fortune 100 company where everyone knew that the senior-most leaders were playing two or three levels below their pay grades and forcing everyone else to do the same. No one ever talked about this, and it just continued. It was so significant that many of the minute details that were "in the weeds" took over for the most strategic discussions about the long-term future of the company that needed to be had.

The image of the senior-most leaders rappelling from the higher positions down into the weeds caught everyone's attention. The entire group couldn't stop focusing on the truth of the imagery. The CEO asked the entire team, "Is this how you see it?" Not only was the answer yes, but one executive captured the consequences of how they were leading perfectly when she stated that "We spend

FIGURE 5.5 *Rappelling into the weeds*

most of our time in the minutia of justifying what happened yester-
day, instead of the key prep work of what we want to have happen
tomorrow!" The meetings, habits, and routines that perpetuated the
"in-the-weeds" behaviors changed and ushered in some of the most
significant and successful culture and business changes the company had experienced.

Example 3: I Meet My Number
So I Can Play by My Own Rules

As for the next company, the hidden truth that was circling was if
you hit your stretch budget number, you could do whatever you
wanted. And once that happened, the new rules for the enterprise
strategy, culture, and change process didn't apply to you. Yet no
one was talking about this truth in public. It took a simple cartoon
(Figure 5.6) and a short statement to unleash a torrent of questions
about the future of the business and the necessity of everyone to

FIGURE 5.6 *Playing by my own rules*

be aligned on its strategy. The enterprise strategy wasn't optional, and the "favoritism" of making it optional for leaders who delivered quarterly stretch financial numbers stopped immediately after the cartoon served up the issue. The strategy and change agenda became the same for all.

Willingness to Engage with the Truth

These are just a few examples that highlight some of the key issues that we see leadership teams struggle with and where it doesn't feel safe to tell the truth. The longer the items go unaddressed, the more detrimental they tend to be to the effectiveness of the team. As a leader, you have to assume that the natural forces of a large organization work against a truth-telling environment. With that in mind, good leaders continually focus on removing truth-telling barriers and creating an environment where it feels safe for people to tell them what they really think and feel.

What it does require is vulnerability by the leader, as not all truths are reinforcing, comforting, or good news. But the willingness to engage with the truth is in and of itself a sign of being a strong and bold leader.

The Art of Having Truthful Conversations

If you want to jump-start a truth-telling environment, consider the following 45-minute activity with your team. We call it "Walls of Greatness and Reality," and the activity begins with a discussion of what we are good at and then moves to what we are not so good at.

Follow the steps below to complete the activity:

1. Give each team member three or four large Post-it Notes. Ask each of the members to write down one item per note that is great about the team and how it has worked together and executed in the past 12 months.

2. Have the team members place each of these on an open wall space and start to "affinity-group" them (Figure 5.7). Line up the various notes that fit under the same theme. You should end up with numerous vertical rows of key themes.

FIGURE 5.7 *Affinity-group notes by theme.*

3. Have team members alternate reading all the notes aloud and provide any commentary they see fit. At the end, ask the group for the story that describes what the team is great at. Capture the "Wall of Greatness" story on a flipchart.

4. Repeat the activity by giving everyone another three or four large Post-it Notes and ask each person to write down where the team has the greatest opportunities or disconnects.

5. Place these notes on a different space on the wall. Repeat the activity of affinity-grouping the notes and reading the vertical columns aloud with the team standing in front of the wall.

6. Ask the team members to put a check mark by the three issues they each believe are most relevant and represent the greatest opportunity for the team.

7. Identify the two or three key themes that emerge from the group.

8. Ask the following questions:
    a. Why do you think these realities exist?
    b. How have we helped create these realities?
    c. How have we personally benefited from these realities?
    d. What can we do to make sure our Wall of Reality looks different six months from now?

Questions b and c require vulnerability, and it can be very powerful if the leader goes first. Either way, this activity will give you quick insight into how comfortable your team is in talking about difficult issues.

From Walls of Greatness and Reality to Truth Statements

One question that we are often asked after revealing a sketch or a Wall of Reality is, "How do you use these to help teams, cultures, and organizations tell the truth and get better?"

First, we work with our clients to decide on the visual sketches and quotes that are most real or relevant and are truly holding the organization back from becoming what it is capable of. We ask teams to translate the truest images into "truth statements" about what they are dissatisfied with and want to change. We explain that these truth statements are as hard-hitting as the truth is, and that when the team members look at them, they cannot be comfortable with the idea of doing nothing to address them. At the end of the session, they agree that they will keep looking at the truth statements until they feel that the statements no longer accurately describe the current realities and truths. Most teams generate 7 to 10 truth statements after looking at their humorous sketches about the realities that they are slow to acknowledge and address. Here are five examples from different companies that still stick out for us as much today as the day they were first crafted by the members of the team telling each other the truth.

It should be noted and shouted from the highest mountain that each of the companies behind the five truth statements below made major changes to address the unflattering statements and had dramatic changes in performance—so dramatic that they often went from the last to first quartile in performance within two years from first telling themselves the truth and deciding to do something about it.

Sample Truth Statements

1. *We do not probe our business for performance, and as a result we don't know the difference between good and lucky in our 28 divisions.* (Home builder)

2. *We claim that we are customer obsessed, but we are finance obsessed, and don't take the controls off our people because if we did, we don't trust*

that they would do the right thing for the customer or the business. (Large restaurant chain)

3. *We do not create stretch-credible targets that are believed and owned through execution by our people.* (Industrial manufacturer)

4. *We say we are all about being a people company, but we rarely prioritize developing people, we don't like doing it, and when we do it we aren't very good at it.* (Food service company)

5. *The world today moves in "nanoseconds," and we are using the agrarian calendar of seasons as our pace determiner, and as a result, we aren't meeting the current needs of our patients, physicians, or associates.* (Healthcare system)

USING YOUR TOOLS

The tools and processes laid out in this chapter will help you to create an environment of truth telling. But more than anything else, what is required is an authentic commitment to create a culture where people feel safe. Your employees must feel comfortable telling you what they really think and feel. Truth is a critical blind spot that can create an environment of poor decision making mixed with a significant lack of trust and disengagement in your organization.

If you don't make the effort to allow truth to guide your teams, the true problems of your organization and the best ideas of your employees will remain buried in the hearts and minds of your people. Let your employees speak candidly and you will have an organization that soars.

CHAPTER SIX

Assessing Your Leadership Blind Spots and Lessons Learned

ASSESSING YOUR LEADERSHIP BLIND SPOTS

As you read the previous chapters, you were likely thinking about whether purpose, story, engagement, trust, and truth are leadership blind spots for you or your organization or possibly with how you lead. One of the goals we had for this book was to provide an easy way for readers to objectively assess if any of these leadership blind spots are present in their organization.

We have a team of master's- and doctorate-level researchers at Root Inc. whose sole job is to conduct quantitative and qualitative research. They help organizations uncover blind spots on all kinds of people-related issues, from the most important touchpoints that shape a great client experience to the leadership behaviors that support a desired culture. We sat down with that team and worked through the core drivers that create the five leadership blind spots that appear in this book.

With those identified and with your deeper understanding of the five leadership blind spots, we have created a 10-minute assessment that provides a snapshot of the strengths and weaknesses that may exist within your organization as they relate to these leadership blind spots. The final product is what you will work through over the pages that follow.

Our hope is that the insights you gain from this assessment open the door to new conversations and approaches that allow you to be a better leader, have a more effective and engaged team, and ultimately create a more successful organization. If you are not in a leadership position, we hope this information creates awareness and leads to a conversation on where and how you can improve.

As you take the assessment, think of your organization or business unit as your primary reference point. Read each of the 21 statements and rate how strongly you agree or disagree.

FIVE BLIND SPOTS ASSESSMENT

Using the seven-point scale provided, please rate your level of agreement with each of the following statements.

		Strongly Disagree						Strongly Agree
		1	2	3	4	5	6	7
1.	Our purpose is a meaningful guide in our strategic planning and decision making.							
2.	Our purpose is unique and expresses our organization's desired impact on the world.							
3.	In our organization, we see our purpose as a key driver of our profits.							
4.	Purpose is equally important to us in good times and in bad.							
5.	We have a vision statement that clearly describes what winning looks like.							
6.	We have a strategy story that creates a sense of adventure our people are excited about.							
7.	If I ask each member of the team to draw our strategy story, the pictures will look very similar.							
8.	Leaders share our strategy story consistently and effectively.							
9.	We have a vision statement that uniquely sets us apart from competitors.							
10.	We frequently engage our people in conversations about our most important business matters.							

	Strongly Disagree						Strongly Agree
	1	2	3	4	5	6	7
11. We emphasize both the rational and emotional aspects of our story when engaging our people.							
12. We actively encourage our people to think through the challenges and opportunities of our business.							
13. We invite our people to use their unique talents to help differentiate us with customers.							
14. Our people understand that our expectations include knowing when to follow firm rules and knowing when to use their best judgment.							
15. Our organization encourages people to think outside the box and take calculated risks rather than being safe and sticking to the rules.							
16. We trust our people to develop and implement innovative ideas that can improve our business.							
17. Our leaders create an environment where it is safe for people to say what they think and feel.							
18. Our leaders want to hear the truth, even if the truth is bad.							
19. The real conversations in our organization take place out in the open during meetings rather than in private.							
20. Our leaders are vulnerable about themselves and what they need to change.							
21. In our organization, our people are empowered to use their strengths without fear of retribution or penalty.							

With the assessment completed, let's see how you did.

FIVE BLIND SPOTS ASSESSMENT SCORING

Instructions: *The questions on the assessment align with the five leadership blind spots as outlined in the chart below. Please add the total for each category and write the score in the appropriate box. For example, the first four questions in the assessment relate to the "Purpose" blind spot. If your total score for the first four questions equals 20, write "20" in the middle box of the Purpose row below.*

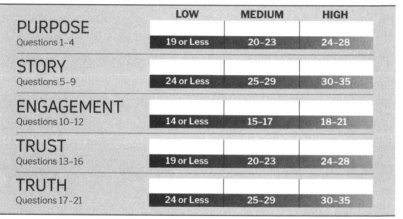

	LOW	MEDIUM	HIGH
PURPOSE Questions 1–4	19 or Less	20–23	24–28
STORY Questions 5–9	24 or Less	25–29	30–35
ENGAGEMENT Questions 10–12	14 or Less	15–17	18–21
TRUST Questions 13–16	19 or Less	20–23	24–28
TRUTH Questions 17–21	24 or Less	25–29	30–35

Add your scores from each blind spot

_____ + _____ + _____ + _____ + _____ = _____
PURPOSE   STORY   ENGAGEMENT   TRUST   TRUTH

Your Leadership Blind Spot Gut Check	
Congratulations. You have no real leadership blind spots in your organization. Keep it up!	**117–147**
You have some strengths but also some opportunity areas that need attention.	**105–116**
Things aren't falling apart, but there are numerous leadership blind spots that need to be addressed.	**84–104**
You are in some leadership trouble, and it is only a matter of time before it catches up with you.	Less than **84**

There are two ways to look at your scores to determine what course of action may be worth taking. One is your overall score and judging whether you are operating from a position of strength or from a position of weakness as it relates to your leadership blind spots.

If your average score was 105 or higher, you are largely operating from a position of strength. The leaders in your organization are savvy and self-aware about some of the essential leadership traits that breed success. You should feel good about the long-term direction of the company and its ability to be agile and successful and to create an environment that people want to be a part of. There are likely some opportunity areas, but you are looking to tweak, refine, and build on strengths that are deeply embedded in your leadership DNA.

If your score is 104 or less, you likely have leadership challenges you need to work on. Even if things are going well within your business today, your ability to adapt and be flexible, to work through the unexpected, and to connect with your people if substantial change happens is a significant concern. Leadership weakness often doesn't fully show up until an organization is hit with a crisis or is in need of radical change or transformation. Your summary score gives you an indication of how well you will be able to lead through a big change when it comes your way.

The second way to look at your scores is to analyze how you did in each of the five leadership blind spots and where you are in the low, medium, or high categories on the scoring sheet. It is helpful to be clear on strengths you can build on, or on the flip side, if there are one or two leadership blind spots that are holding you back from being great.

Keep in mind that this score only reflects your perception of the leadership blind spots that exist within your organization or your team. You will get a broader and more meaningful view if you get the perspective of several people and compare results. This assessment is available online if you have a desire for you, your team, or your organization to get a snapshot view of how you are doing on these leadership blind spots. In addition, we have some larger normative data available that will give you a sense of how you compare with other organizations. If any of your scores raises a yellow or red flag about any of the leadership blind spots, we have created an additional resource section on our website that provides tips and tricks to work through and improve any leadership blind spot you might have. To access this information, visit http://www.rootinc.com/leaderblindspots.

LESSONS LEARNED

In working with organizations of all sizes and in dozens of countries around the world, we have discovered lessons from the "University of the Streets" where leaders are faced with real engagement challenges and experience tremendous success. These lessons are embedded throughout each chapter. Our goal in this chapter is to provide a quick guide or antidote for each of the five leadership blind spots that hold back people and organizations from being the very best versions of themselves every day. Each of the 13 "lessons learned" represents an action leaders can take to invigorate the power of all human beings in their organizations to get engaged, make valuable contributions, and deliver value for the people they serve. If there is a common theme that runs throughout the lessons learned, it is the importance of creating connections between the people in our organizations and the tremendous hunger they have for genuine conversation. It is our hope that our 13 lessons learned about leadership, leadership beliefs, and the impact they have on people can be a starting point for you to examine your own beliefs and behaviors.

If you think back to the Introduction, we highlighted several shocking practices from the past that seem just too outrageous to be true—practices such as druggists selling cocaine drops to give to kids with a toothache, doctors advertising the health benefits of smoking, or a soda company advocating for the practice of lacing your baby formula with a carbonated soft drink. They really happened, and many of today's common leadership practices are just as out of date when it comes to our overall approach to tapping the dormant talent and spirit of our people.

We encourage you to stop for a moment, consider your assessment from above, and think about which of the blind spots apply to you. Reconsider your assumptions, your mindset, and your leadership practices. Here are 13 ways that you can get started.

Leadership Blind Spot Lessons: Purpose

1. **Make purpose personal.** People have a natural desire to be a part of something bigger than themselves. No one can inspire that feeling and connection more than the leaders of an organization. Not only do people process what a purpose says and represents, but they look at the leaders of an organization to see if they authentically live and represent that purpose. Is it something leaders have a personal connection with? Do they talk about it in formal and informal settings? Is it something a leader acts on when no one is looking?

    When people see leaders meaningfully connect and lead with purpose, it gives people permission to do the same while inspiring greater meaning, belief, and action for all. Being clear, passionate, and public on "why you do what you do" may be the most powerful motivational tool for your people.

2. **Be passionate about your purpose, not your numbers.** Numbers are an essential part of success in any business. They tell us whether what we do is truly resonating with customers. But they need to be an outcome of purpose-driven goals, and yet for many organizations, they represent the end in and of itself. When leaders are upside down about this, meetings, presentations, and leaders revolve around numbers.

The most effective leaders constantly inspire and have their teams focus on purpose-driven strategies. The core organizational energy is spent on how what we do creates unique value for our customers, sets us apart from the competition, improves the employee experience, or enhances the community we live in and serve.

Numbers tell us about the progress we are making on those ambitions, but they are not the ambitions themselves.

Leadership Blind Spot Lessons: Story

3. **Proactively close the gap between what we say and what we mean.** One of the most obvious ways leadership teams can improve is to eliminate their superficial alignment on critical strategic issues. While people on a team tend to nod their heads in agreement when discussions turn to being "more efficient," "innovative," or "digitally enabled," the truth is that team members often lack shared meaning of how these types of things truly come to life, what the trade-offs are, and what resources they will require.

    There is a significant gap between the words we use and a true sense of shared meaning of what those words represent in terms of mindsets, behaviors, and activities.

4. **Don't let your stories kill your strategies.** We all remember great stories. They may be from our favorite films or books, teachers who taught us a new way to think, or coaches who inspired us to accomplish something extraordinary.

    Stories have the power to meaningfully connect, inspire, and create change, and yet most leaders don't lead with stories that inspire and connect the dots. Instead they lead with data, slides, and bullets that lack a compelling narrative. And even if the narrative is solid, we frequently see leaders struggle to tell the story in a compelling way. You can be sitting on the greatest strategic plan in the world, but if you can't frame a compelling story so people want to be a part of it, you will struggle to implement it.

5. **Don't place foolish emphasis on WIIFM.** One of the first questions we get from clients who are thinking about significant change is "What's in it for me (WIIFM)?" We need to answer this for people, or they will not want to be a part of the change. Yet while that is certainly an important question to gain clarity on, we have found that engaging people in the adventure and possibilities of what can be created together is even more important.

The saying that the journey is as important as the destination holds true for many people in the workplace. Most people have a desire to complete more than a set of tasks when at work. They want to have a sense of belonging and know that their contributions make a meaningful difference. When people are assured of this, the likelihood that they will put forth discretionary energy and help lead the change increases exponentially.

In the end, being challenged, finding a better way, and contributing to something that makes a difference are just as important as the answer to "WIIFM."

Leadership Blind Spot Lessons: Engagement

6. **Focus on the emotional versus the rational.** When organizations manage change, they almost inevitably gather all the critical facts, prepare extensive communication plans to share those facts, and then are frustrated when nothing changes. We then often hear that "our people don't get it" and "they don't want to change."

The starting point to achieve meaningful change is to get a sense of what the members of your target audience think and feel and to provide them an opportunity to be heard. If you can't find a way to your employees' hearts, their minds won't follow.

Most organizations operate with the fundamental belief that leading with good rationale creates change, but the reality is, it requires making an emotional connection with your people first.

7. **Use dialogue to reach the hearts and minds of your people.** Whatever we accomplish in our work, there may be nothing more precious than feeling that we truly matter. This can happen through authentic workplace dialogue. Dialogue is more than just ordinary conversation. The purpose of dialogue is to understand others and not just share our independent views.

    Dialogue opens our hearts and minds because it creates close connections between caring, listening, questioning, refining new ideas, and finding better solutions. Dialogue is the living experience of inquiry within and between people. It seeks to value and harness the collective intelligence of people on a team or in an organization.

    Thinking with others to mine our collective expertise, challenging long-held assumptions, and improving upon ideas for a better future are all only possible with dialogue. It is the only path to engage the hearts and minds of people.

8. **Flip the switch for your people.** Authentic conversations often leave leaders dumbfounded at the untapped intelligence of their people. The key is to take the challenges of the business to your people instead of answering these questions for them or robotically instructing them to execute your answers. Those of us closest to the work are the experts. We each want to solve our own puzzles.

    People are energized by being asked about their opinions and ideas to help solve any organization's most pressing problems. The experiences and observations of employees are grossly underleveraged in most organizations. Elevate your expectations of what your people are capable of and flip the switch—then watch the lights shine brightly.

Leadership Blind Spot Lessons: Trust

9. **Embrace human variability rather than reduce it.** For processes like Lean and Six Sigma, it is valuable to eliminate human variability, but this approach doesn't work when it comes to tapping the human spirit, optimizing discretionary effort, and creating unique experiences for fellow employees and customers. Instead the goal should be to add human variability and judgment that create exceptional performances.

    Nurturing and encouraging the judgment of our people creates the conditions for everyone to contribute their best selves. Nurturing and encouraging the judgment of our people is the ultimate differentiator.

10. **Clarify hard lines, guidelines, and no lines to make the complex simple.** "Centralized or decentralized?" and "control or freedom?" are not the right questions when it comes to engaging your people. Control and trust—or as we call it, framework and freedom—require better instructions for people to comprehend exactly what is expected of them.

    At first glance, the concepts of control and trust seem to be opposite and in conflict. However, they are complementary if you truly understand how they each apply to employee engagement and strategy execution. The question should be, "When do we use a consistent company standard, and when should people use their unique judgment, care, and discretion?"

    The way to simplify instructions of both control and trust is to adopt the terminology of hard lines, guidelines, and no lines. *Hard lines* are the areas where there is one organizational way of doing things with no exceptions. *Guidelines* come with guardrails where the boundaries are firm, but how things get done between the guardrails is up to the individual. *No lines* means inviting people to use their special talents to do things as they see fit. Using the language of hard lines, guidelines, and no lines is the best way to scale the unique human judgment, discretion, and care of our people, while still having firm standards that we all share.

Leadership Blind Spot Lessons: Truth

11.   **Use humor: It's not just funny; it's breakthrough.** Humor creates an environment where it's safe to tell the truth. It is not only a method to make someone laugh but also a safe way to show the facts, lay your cards on the table, and enable people to say what they think and feel.

   Saturday Night Live has made a living doing that with political skits for the past 30 years. It is also a very effective method that has been used in the *Dilbert* cartoons to serve up painful and challenging work issues that we know to be true. Humor can be used to tell the truth in a disarming and safe way that makes it easier to talk about difficult challenges without the conversation being so personal that it indicts us as the problem. It helps each of us not to take ourselves too seriously.

   Making good use of humor reduces the hostilities of truth and gets rid of the embarrassment that keeps most people from embracing it.

12.   **Create a truth-telling culture.** Hard-hitting truth statements about the realities of what people are "dissatisfied with" but believe are unsafe to discuss can be the starting point for people to go from a victim mentality to one of co-accountability.

   Creating public alignment on the truths that most hold an organization back can create a shared view of today's most important realities. Addressing these truths head-on and creating vulnerability by asking each team member to identify how he or she has contributed to these truths will open the door to the realization that we have control of many of the things we frequently complain about.

13. **To thyself be true and others will follow.** For any leader, confidence is a key ingredient to success. However, an over-active ego makes it difficult for the truth to show up in any setting. When leaders are genuinely curious about the truth and willing to set their egos aside to find it, the truth often shows up on our doorstep. Realism is at the heart of authentic engagement.

Practice humility, seek out your own truth tellers (or court jesters), and remind yourself that the work is not about you. Instead it is about the people you serve, what they truly feel, and what they need to be successful.

A FINAL COMMENT

The lessons above can be transformative for your leadership and are the launching pads to create and sustain exceptional results. In our experience, people don't resist change; they resist being changed by someone else. Authentically engage their hearts and minds, and amazing results will follow. The fact that 70 percent of people who come to work every day are not engaged, not inspired, don't feel safe to say what they think and feel, and wait until they go home to contribute their best self is stunning and unacceptable. As leaders, it is a business and morale issue that we must change.

We hope in some small way we have started you on the path to make the five leadership blind spots as obsolete as cocaine drops are now for children who have toothaches!

Notes

Introduction

1. Vibul V. Vadakan, "The Asphyxiating and Exsanguinating Death of President George Washington," *The Permanente Journal*, Vol. 8, No. 2, Spring 2004, pp. 76–79, http://www.thepermanentejournal.org/files/Spring2004/time.pdf.
2. Howard Markel, "Dec. 14, 1799: The Excruciating Final Hours of President George Washington," *PBS Newshour*, December 14, 2004, http://www.pbs.org/newshour/updates/dec-14-1799-excruciating-final-hours-president-george-washington/.
3. Gerry Greenstone, "The History of Bloodletting," *BC Medical Journal*, Vol. 52, No. 1, January/February 2010, pp. 12–14, http://www.bcmj.org/premise/history-bloodletting.
4. Jennie Cohen, "A Brief History of Bloodletting," History.com, A&E Television Networks, May 30, 2012, http://www.history.com/news/a-brief-history-of-bloodletting.
5. Rupal Parekh, "Rewind: '50s Era 7UP Campaign Depicted Soda-Guzzling Babies," *AdAge*, August 27, 2012, http://adage.com/article/news/rewind-50s-era-7up-campaign-depicted-soda-guzzling-babies/236867/.
6. Robert Kaplan and David Norton, *The Strategy-Focused Organization: How Balanced Scorecard Companies Thrive in the New Business Environment*, Harvard Business School Press, 2000.
7. "State of the American Workplace," Gallup, July 2017, http://news.gallup.com/reports/199961/state-american-workplace-report-2017.aspx.

Chapter 1

1. Sam Ro, "Stock Market Investors Have Become Absurdly Impatient," *Business Insider Australia,* August 8, 2012, https://www.businessinsider.com.au/stock-investor-holding -period-2012-8.

2. "The State of the Debate on Purpose in Business," EY Beacon Institute, EYGM Limited, 2016, p. 13, http://www.ey.com/ Publication/vwLUAssets/ey-the-state-of-the-debate-on -purpose-in-business/$FILE/ey-the-state-of-the-debate-on -purpose-in-business.pdf.

3. Raj Sisodia, David B. Wolfe, and Jag Sheth, *Firms of Endearment: How World-Class Companies Profit from Passion and Purpose,* 2nd ed., Pearson FT Press, 2014.

4. Greg Satell, "A Look Back at Why Blockbuster Really Failed and Why It Didn't Have to," *Forbes,* September 5, 2014, https:// www.forbes.com/sites/gregsatell/2014/09/05/a-look-back-at -why-blockbuster-really-failed-and-why-it-didnt-have-to/ #6f193a681d64.

5. David Reiss, "4 Lessons from Blockbuster Failure," February 25, 2015, LinkedIn, https://www.linkedin.com/pulse/4-lessons -from-blockbuster-failure-david-reiss/.

6. "Public Trust in Government: 1958–2017," Pew Research Center, May 3, 2017, http://www.people-press.org/2017/05/03/ public-trust-in-government-1958-2017/.

7. Steve Denning, "Salesforce CEO Slams 'The World's Dumbest Idea': Maximizing Shareholder Value," *Forbes,* February 5, 2015, https://www.forbes.com/sites/stevedenning/2015/02/05/ salesforce-ceo-slams-the-worlds-dumbest-idea-maximizing -shareholder-value/#2079c5b87883.

8. "We Quit Tobacco, Here's What Happened Next," CVS Health, https://cvshealth.com/thought-leadership/cvs-health-research -institute/we-quit-tobacco-heres-what-happened-next.

9. Bruce Jones, "The Disney Institute: Mission Versus Purpose: What's the Difference?" Disney Institute, April 23, 2015, https://disneyinstitute.com/blog/2015/04/mission-versus -purpose-whats-the-difference/.

10. Simon Sinek, *Start with Why: How Great Leaders Inspire Everyone to Take Action,* reprint edition, Portfolio, 2011.

Chapter 2

1. Janet Rae-Dupree, "Innovative Minds Don't Think Alike," *New York Times*, December 30, 2007.
2. Stephen Denning, "Telling Tales," *Harvard Business Review*, May 2004.
3. Maria Popova, "The Psychology of What Makes a Great Story," Brain Pickings, https://www.brainpickings.org/2016/01/20/jerome-bruner-actual-minds-possible-worlds-storytelling/.
4. Moni Basu, "The Importance of Effective Storytelling and the Dangers of PowerPoint," CNN, September 17, 2011.
5. Tim Pollard, *The Compelling Communicator*, Conder House Press, 2016. Section is from Chapter 1.

Chapter 3

1. Edward Tufte, *Wired Magazine*, September 1, 2003.
2. Lori Goler, Janelle Gale, Brynn Harrington, and Adam Grant, "The 3 Things Employees Really Want: Career, Community, Cause," *Harvard Business Review*, February 20, 2018, https://hbr.org/2018/02/people-want-3-things-from-work-but-most-companies-are-built-around-only-one.
3. Alan Deutschman, *Change or Die*, HarperCollins, 2007.
4. William Isaacs, *Dialogue and the Art of Thinking Together*, Doubleday division of Randomhouse, 1999.
5. Daniel Yankelovich, *The Magic of Dialogue*,

Chapter 4

1. Alex Ihnen, "MythBusters Tackles Four-Way Stop v. Roundabout Traffic Throughput," nextSTL, Next Media, October 9, 2013, https://nextstl.com/.../mythbusters-tackles-four-way-stop-v-roundabout-traffic-throughput/.

2.   Rob Wile, "Here's How Much United Airlines Stock Tanked This
      Week," *Money*, April 14, 2017, http://time.com/money/4739880/
      united-airlines-fiasco-overbooked-passenger-dragged-stock
      -price-value/.
3.   Tara Allen, "Rules vs. Values-Based Cultures," March 24, 2015,
      LinkedIn, https://www.linkedin.com/pulse/rules-vs-values
      -based-cultures-tara-allen/.
4.   Tasha Eurich, "CEO Disease," *Chief Learning Officer*, May 24,
      2017.

Chapter 5

1.   Christine Comaford, "63% of Employees Don't Trust Their
      Leader—Here's What You Can Do to Change That," Forbes.com,
      Forbes Media LLC, January 27, 2017, https://www.forbes.com/
      sites/christinecomaford/2017/01/28/63-of-employees-dont
      -trust-their-leader-heres-what-you-can-do-to-change-that/.
2.   Kathleen Blanchard, "Power Robs the Brain of Empathy," *Digital
      Journal*, August 10, 2015, http://www.digitaljournal.com/
      article/356229.
3.   Jon Simmons, "How to Get Over Your Fear of Speaking Up at
      Work," Monster.com, https://www.monster.com/career-advice/
      article/how-to-get-over-fear-speaking-up-at-work.

Index

Action
    organizational purpose in, 18–20
    for personal purpose, 20–21
    for purpose-driven organization,
      1, 4–6, 13, 20
    for storytelling, 46–48
Acute ascending aortic dissection,
    Type 1, 19–20
Advantage, over competition, 10–11,
    76
Adventure, in business, 26, 32, 37–38,
    39–40
Advisory Committee Report on
    Smoking and Health (Surgeon
    General, U.S.) (1964), xiv–xv
Affinity-grouping, 131
Alignment
    of strategy story, 49–51, 143
    of words, 48–50, 143
Allen, Tara, 86–87
Amazon, 35
Apple, 12, 14, 87
Appreciation, of employees, xxiv–xxv,
    19–20
Aristotle, xiii
Assessment, of blind spots, 135,
    136–141
    worksheet for, 137–139
Audience, 41
    connection with, 54–56

Authentic
    conversations, 60, 110, 123–125
    dialogue culture, 61–62, 65–70,
      110, 145
    engagement, 75–76, 148
    story, 42–43
Auto industry, 39–40

Beliefs. *See also* Past beliefs
    about business, 29–31
    challenge of, xviii, xix
    changing, xix–xx
    of leadership, xx–xxi, xxv, 3–4, 76,
      78–79, 83, 103
Blame, in organizations, 74, 75
Blind spots, xviii, xx–xxii, xxix–xxx,
    54–55. *See also* Engagement;
    Purpose; Story; Trust; Truth
    assessment of, 135, 136–141
    drivers of, 136, 137–138
    lessons learned about, 141–148
Blockbuster, 7–8
Bloodletting, xii
Brand Compass, of Hampton, 98–99
Brand loyalty, 9–10, 13, 104
Brion, Arden, 19–20
Bruner, Jerome, 32
Built to Last (Collins and Porras), 6–7
Business. *See also* Organizations
    adventure in, 26, 32, 37–38, 39–40

Business (*continued*)
  differentiation of, xxiii–xxix, 77,
    97–98, 105
  growth of, 25–26, 82
  metrics of, xxvi, xxvii, 1, 3–5
Business schools, xix, 4

The Canyon, 71–75
CEO. *See* Chief Intelligence Officer
Challenge
  of beliefs, xviii, xix
  purpose as, 4–5, 10
Change
  in auto industry, 39–40
  of beliefs, xix–xx
  embracing, 8, 38
  leadership facilitating, xxii, 5, 10,
    13, 16, 58–59, 82
  truth telling as catalyst for,
    113–114, 127, 133
Change or Die (Deutschman), 58–59
Chief Intelligence Officer (CEO), 3–4,
    12, 43, 48, 49, 89, 108, 110–111,
    119
Childhood obesity, xvi–xvii
Cocaine as medicine, xiii–xiv, 141–142,
    148
Collective wisdom, from dialogue, 63,
    66, 69–70, 74–75, 145
Collins, Jim, 6–7
Communication
  effectiveness in, 45–48
  PowerPoint for, xxviii, 38–39, 44
The Compelling Communicator
    (Pollard), 46–47
Competition, xxi, xxiii, 8
  advantage over, 10–11, 76
  Blockbuster and, 7–8
  technology and, 7, 39
Connection
  with audience, 54–56
  with customer, 120
Conscious Capitalism forum, 7
Consequences, of financial crisis,
    8–10
Control and trust, 87–89, 90–93, 102,
    105

Control way vs. trust way, 77, 78–82,
    83–90, 99, 103
Conversations
  creating authentic, 60, 110,
    123–125
  rules for, 65–71
  vignettes for, 127–130
Conviction, of purpose, 13, 20
Cook, Tim, 12
Cordell, Phil, 100–101
Corporations, trust in, 9–10, 13
Co-thinking, 61, 65, 69–70, 75–76
Creation
  of conversations and dialogue,
    60–62, 65–70, 110, 123–125,
    145
  of engagement, 59–60, 76
  of framework and freedom, 90,
    93–94, 101
  of happiness, 14, 21
  of personal purpose, 25–28
  of purpose-driven organization, 3,
    5–6, 10, 11–13, 14–18
  of story, 29, 41–43, 47–48
  of truth telling culture, 107, 108,
    109–113, 118–119, 121–124,
    130–134, 147
Customers
  connection with, 120
  purpose and, 6, 8, 9–10, 12–13, 23
  service to, 7–8, 102–105
CVS, 12–13

Dao, David, 85–86
Data, xxi
  on employee candor, 108
  on purpose-driven organization, 7
  on trusting people, 84–85
  on truth telling, 108
  on use of visuals, 50
Davis, Sammy, Jr., xv
Demand, for purpose-driven organi-
    zation, 10–11
Denning, Stephen, 31–32, 38
Detert, James, 115
Deutschman, Alan, 58–59
Diabetes, xvi

Dialogue and the Art of Thinking Together (Issacs), 61–62
Dialogue culture
    as authentic, 61–62, 65–70, 110, 145
    The Canyon and, 71–75
    collective wisdom through, 63, 66, 69–70, 74–75, 145
    as engaging, 60–70
    "Model for Dialogue," 60–65
    Socratic questions, small groups and visuals for, 65–70
    use of visuals for, 68–70, 71, 74–75
Differentiation, xxiii–xxix, 77, 97–98, 105
Dilbert (cartoon), 110, 122
Disengagement
    excitement vs., xxvi, 59–60
    PowerPoint creating, 53, 55–56
    in strategy story, 45–46
Disney, Walt, 14
Disneyland, 14
Disruption, of market, 7–8
Doctors. *See* Physicians
Dream
    of King, Jr., 46–48
    as purpose, 14
Drivers
    of blind spots, 136, 137–138
    of engagement, 57–62
Driving Excellence (Allen), 86–87
Dunkin' Donuts, 103

Economic recession. *See* Financial crisis (2008-2009)
Economic value added (EVA), xxiii
Edelman Trust Barometer, 67, 108
Effectiveness
    in communication, 45–48
    of strategy story, 30–31, 41
Elements, for trust, 82
Embracement
    of change, 8, 38
    of risk, 25, 26, 59
Emotional connection, for engage-ment, 57–59, 74–75, 144–145
Empathy, in framework and freedom, 94–96

Employees
    as appreciative, xxiv–xxv, 19–20
    business reputation and, 102–103
    candor of, 108
    engagement of, xx–xxi, xxiv–xxvii, 2, 5–6, 15, 53, 55–59, 94–95, 145
    inspiring, xxvi, 16, 20–21
    investment in, 13, 101–102
    ownership by, xxix, 59, 80–82, 88, 101–102, 107
    potential of, 15, 18, 76, 83, 97–98
    purpose connected to, 11–13, 14, 16, 91
    as robots, 83
    story connection with, 30–32, 40–41, 44–46, 144
    value of, xxv–xxvi, 70, 75–76
Engagement, xxv, xxviii, 53
    blind spots in, xxv, xxviii, 53, 144–145
    co-thinking and, 61, 65, 69–70, 75–76
    creating, 59–60, 76
    through dialogue, 60–70
    drivers of, 57–62
    emotional vs. rational, 57–59, 74–75, 144–145
    of employees, xx–xxi, xxiv–xxvii, 2, 5–6, 15, 53, 55–59, 94–95, 145
    Gallup poll on, xxi
    hope through, 58–59
    inspiring authentic, 75–76, 148
    leadership role in, xxii, 2, 30, 55, 60–62
    metrics linked to, 57, 80–81
    strategy for, 53
    through strategy story, 29, 30–31, 37–41, 44, 46
    trust and, 67, 80–81
    through vision statement, 33, 35, 37–38
Era of transparency, 102–103
Essentials, of story creation, 41–45
Eurich, Tasha, 119
EVA. *See* Economic value added

Examples
    of dialogue power, 71–75
    of framework and freedom,
        93–101
    of past beliefs, xiii–xviii, 141–142,
        148
    of vision statement, 34, 36
Excitement
    disengagement vs., xxvi, 59–60
    about purpose, 18, 20, 21
    for strategy story, 30, 37, 38–40, 46
Experience economy, xx
Experiment, tappers vs. listeners, 30

Fear, xxiv
    "force, facts, and fear," 58–59
    of truth telling, 108–109, 111–112,
        113–114, 115–119, 122, 125
Financial crisis (2008–2009),
        soul-searching during, 8–9, 10
Firms of Endearment (Sisodia, Wolfe,
        Sheth), 7
Followership, inspiration creating, 38
"force, facts, and fear," 58–59
Framework and freedom, 87–89,
        90–101
    creating culture of, 90, 93–94, 101
    creativity in, 80–82, 86–87, 89–90,
        92, 99, 103–105
    examples of, 93–101
    Hampton way, 96–101
    hard lines, guidelines, and no
        lines, 92–93, 96, 98, 146–147
    in healthcare, 94–96
    implementation of, 90–94, 96
France, Van Arsdale, 14
Freedom. See Framework and
    freedom

Gain-sharing, xxiv
Gallup poll, xxi
Game-changing results, 13, 21, 25, 62
Goler, Lori, 57
Grant, Amy, 54
Growth, of business, 25–26, 82
Guidelines, purpose statement,
        14–16, 22–23

Hampton, by Hilton, 104
    Brand Compass of, 98–99
    framework and freedom in,
        96–101
    Hamptonality, 96, 98–100
Happiness, creating, 14, 21
Hard lines, guidelines, and no lines,
        92–93, 96, 98, 146–147
Headline, vision statement as, 32–33,
        37–38
Healthcare, in framework and
        freedom, 94–96
Hippocrates, xii
Hope
    in engagement, 58–59
    in truth telling, 112–113
Horn, Robert E., 50
"How Great Leaders Inspire Action"
        (Sinek), 11
Human capital, xxvi
Humor, for truth telling, 110,
        122–124, 147
Humors, in humans, xii

"I Have a Dream" (King, Jr.), 46–48
Ikea, 35
Impact, of purpose-driven organi-
        zation, 15–16, 19–20, 23–24,
        26–27
Implementation
    of framework and freedom,
        90–94, 96
    of purpose statement, 24, 28
Increase, in revenue, 2, 78–82
Indifference, in workplace, xxi, 18, 19
Innovation, technological, 16, 39
Inspiration
    of employees, xxvi, 16, 20–21
    by leadership, 14, 38, 60, 100,
        101–102
    through organizational purpose,
        16–17
    through story, 35, 48
Investment
    in employees, 13, 101–102
    in stocks, 5
Issacs, William, 61–62

Jackson, Mahalia, 48
Jobs, Steve, 87

King, Martin Luther, Jr., 46–48
Kniberg, Henrik, 84–85

Larry (manager), xxiii–xxv
Leadership
    belief system of, xx–xxi, xxv, 3–4,
        76, 78–79, 83, 103
    blind spots of, xix–xxii, xxvii–xxix
    change facilitated by, xxii, 5, 10,
        13, 16, 58–59, 82
    engagement and, xxii, 2, 30, 55,
        60–62
    inspiration by, 14, 38, 60, 100,
        101–102
    managers vs., 71–74
    presentations by, 55–57
    purpose-driven focus of, 3, 10, 20
    story shared by, 46–48
    strategy storytelling and, 40,
        46–48
    trust fostered by, 80–82, 87, 99
    vision statement by, 33, 38
Leading With Noble Purpose
    (McLeod), 18–19
Lear, Tobias, xi
Lenin, Vladimir, 83
Lessons learned, blind spots,
    141–148
Light bulbs, in people, xxii–xxvii, 97

The Magic of Dialogue (Yankelovich),
    65
Managers vs. leadership, 71–74
Market, disruption of, 7–8
Martin, Dean, xv
McLeod, Lisa Earle, 18–19
Metrics
    of business, xxvi, xxvii, 1, 3–5
    engagement linked to, 57, 80–81
    purpose linked to, 2, 4
Misconceptions, of leadership
    employees not trustworthy, 77–82
    about engagement, 53
    purpose matters, 1, 4

story as compelling, 29–30
    about truth telling, 107
"Model for Dialogue," 60–65
    context, content, and application
        as, 63–64
Money
    meaning contrasted with, 18
    as motivation to work, xx
    as negative story headline, 37–38
    purpose and, 6, 7, 9, 18
Motivation to work, money as, xx

Napkin sketch, 51
Newton, Elizabeth, 30

Operating model, 8
    trust related to, 78–82, 87–90
Organizational purpose, in action,
    18–20
Organizational reality, 71–73
    blame as, 74, 75
Organizations, xix. See also Purpose-
        driven organization
    loyalty to, 9–10, 13, 104
    shareholder focus of, 4, 10
Ownership, by employee, xxix, 59,
    80–82, 88, 101–102, 107

Past beliefs
    cocaine as medicine, xiii–xiv,
        141–142, 148
    smoking is healthy, xiv–xvi, 142
    soft drinks as good, xvi–xviii, 142
Personal purpose, 13, 142
    action for, 20–21
    creating, 25–28
    organizational purpose and,
        20–21, 24–28
    Steve S. and, 24–26
    worksheet for, 26–28
Pew Research Institute, 9
Physicians, xii, xv–xvi, 19, 94
Pollard, Tim, 44–45
Porras, Jerry, 6–7
Post-it Note exercise
    story creation through, 40–41
    for truth telling, 131–132

Potential, of employees, 15, 18, 76, 83, 97–98
Power differential, in truth telling, 114–115
Power of dialogue, The Canyon, 71–75
Power of purpose, 11–13, 14, 21–22
PowerPoint presentations
  for communication, xxviii, 38–39, 44, 46
  as disengaging, 53, 55–56
  Tufte on, 55–56
Presentations, by leaders, 55–57
Pricing trends chart, 68
Profit, purpose contrasted with, 4–9, 12–13, 142–143
Purpose. *See also* Purpose-driven organization
  blind spots in, xxvii, 1, 3, 28, 142–143
  as challenge, 4–5, 10
  conviction in, 13, 20
  customers and, 6, 8, 9–10, 12–13, 23
  dream as, 14
  employee connection to, 11–13, 14, 16, 91
  excitement about, 18, 20, 21
  gut check for, 23
  metrics linked to, 2, 4
  misconception about, 1, 4
  money and, 6, 7, 9, 18
  as powerful, 11–13, 14, 21–22
  profit contrasted with, 4–9, 12–13, 142–143
  rise of, 6–7
  as "soft" endeavor, 4
  strategy and, 2, 5, 8, 13, 16
  testing, 13–14, 21–24
  values-based culture and, 90–91
Purpose statement
  in action, 18–20
  guidelines for, 14–16, 22–23
  implementation of, 24, 28
  organizational, 14–18, 21–24
  of Root Inc., 18
  strength of, 21–23

Purpose-driven organization, xxvii, 142–143
  action for, 1, 4–6, 13, 20
  Blockbuster failure as, 7–8
  competitive advantage of, 10–11
  creating, 3, 5–6, 10, 11–13, 14–18
  data on, 7
  demand for, 10–11
  gut check for, 23
  impact of, 15–16, 19–20, 23–24, 26–27
  inspiration of, 16–17
  leadership focus on, 3, 10, 20
  personal purpose and, 20–21, 24–28
  statement of, 14–18, 21–24
  success of, 4, 6–7, 12–13, 21, 24–25, 28
  true north for, 4, 8, 10, 12, 14
Puzzle solving, 59

Rat Pack, xv
Reputation, employee influence on, 102–103
Results, game-changing, 13, 21, 25, 62
Revenue, 3–9, 12–13
  increasing, 2, 78–82
  lack of trust reducing, 78–80
Risk, 25, 26, 59
Robot, employee as, 83
Root Inc., 15–16, 18, 19, 30, 136
Rules
  for great conversations, 65–71
  values-based culture vs., 86–87, 90–91

Safety, in truth telling, 107, 108–112, 114, 122, 123–124, 130, 134
Schwartz, Barry, xix, 10, 95–96
Scripted behaviors. *See* Control way vs. trust way
Service, to customer, 7–8, 102–105
7-Up, xvii–xviii
Shared meaning, through visualization, 48–52
Shareholder value, 4, 10
  "short-termism" and, 5

Sharing, of story, 45–48
Sheth, Jag, 7
"Short-termism," 5
Sinatra, Frank, xv
Sinek, Simon, 11, 21
Sisodia, Raj, 7
Small-group conversations, for
    dialogue, 66–67, 69
Smith, Adam, xix
Smoking, xiv–xvi, 12–13, 142
Social media, 102–103
Societal blind spots, xviii, xix
Socrates, 65–66
Socratic method, in dialogue, 65–66,
    70
Soft drinks, xvi–xviii, 142
Soul-searching, 8–9, 10
S&P. *See* Standard & Poor's
SpaceX, 35
Standard & Poor's (S&P), 7
Start With Why (Sinek), 21
Steve S. (senior executive), 24–25
Stocks
    investment in, 5
Story. *See also* Storytelling, as strategy
    authenticity of, 42–43
    of auto industry, 39–40
    blind spots in, xxvii–xxviii, 29, 52,
        143–144
    of business beliefs, 29–31
    creating, 29, 41–43, 47–48
    effectiveness of, 30–31, 41
    employee connection to, 30–32,
        40–41, 44–46, 144
    engagement with, 30–31, 37, 44
    excitement about, 30, 37, 38–40,
        46
    headline of, 32–33, 37–38
    inspiration from, 35, 48
    misconception about, 29–30
    shared meaning of, 48–52
Storytelling, as strategy, xxvii–xxviii,
    143–144
    action for, 46–48
    components of, 32
    disengagement with, 45–46
    essentials of, 41–43, 46

King, Jr., dream as, 46–48
    leadership role in, 40, 43–44
    Post-it Note exercise for, 40–41
    template for, 46–47
    vision statement and, 29, 32–33, 38
    visualization for, 48–52
Strategy, xxi
    alignment of, 49–51, 143
    engagement as, 53
    purpose and, 2, 5, 8, 13, 16
Strength, of purpose statement, 21–23
Success
    of purpose-driven organization, 4,
        6–7, 12–13, 21, 24–25, 28
    trust resulting in, 79–82, 83, 85,
        103–105
Sugar, xvii
Surgeon General, U.S., xiv–xv

Tax, xvi
Technology
    competition and, 7, 39
    innovation in, 16, 39
"Telling Tales" (Denning), 31–32, 38
Template, for strategy story, 46–47
Test, of purpose, 13–14, 21–24
"The 3 Things Employees Really
    Want" (Goler), 57
Traffic analogy, for trust, 84–85
Transparency. *See* Era of transparency
Trust, xxv, xxviii–xxix, 146–147
    blind spots in, xxv, xxviii–xxix, 77,
        103–105, 146–147
    control and, 87–89, 90–93, 102, 105
    control vs., 77, 79–82, 83–90, 99,
        103
    of corporations, 9–10, 13
    creative freedom and, 80–82,
        86–87, 89–90, 92, 99, 103–105
    data on, 84–85
    Edelman Trust Barometer, 67, 108
    elements for, 82
    engagement and, 67, 80–81
    leaders fostering, 80–82, 87, 99
    leadership lacking, 77–82
    operating model and, 78–82,
        87–90

Trust (*continued*)
  revenue and, 78–80
  scripted behavior and, 77, 78–80,
    86–88
  success through, 79–82, 83, 85,
    103–105
  traffic analogy for, 84–85
Truth, xxix. *See also* Truth telling
  blind spots in, xxix, 107, 134,
    147–148
Truth telling
  as catalyst for change, 113–114,
    127, 133
  creating culture of, 107, 108,
    109–113, 118–119, 121–124,
    130–134, 147–148
  data on, 108
  fear of, 108–109, 111–112,
    113–114, 115–119, 122, 125
  hope through, 112–113
  humor for, 110, 122–124, 147
  misconception about, 107
  power differential in, 114–115
  safe space for, 107, 108–112, 114,
    122, 123–124, 130, 134
  truth statements for, 132–134
  visualization for, 110, 122–130, 133
  Walls of greatness and reality
    activity, 131–132
  watercooler experience for,
    123–124, 125–127
Tufte, Edward R., 55–56

United Airlines Flight 3411 Incident,
    85–86

Valenti, Gina, 97–101, 105
Value
  of employees, xxv–xxvi, 70, 75–76
  for shareholder, 4, 10
Values-based culture, 112–113
  rules vs., 86–87, 90–91

Vignettes, for conversation, 127–130
Vision statement, 29
  examples of, 34, 36
  leadership and, 33, 38
  as story headline, 32–33, 37–38
Visual blind spots, xix
Visualization
  data on, 50
  for dialogue creation, 68–70, 71,
    74–75
  shared meaning through, 48–52
  in storytelling, 48–52
  for truth telling, 110, 122–130, 133

Walls of greatness and reality, activity
    for, 131–132
  affinity-grouping, 131
Washington, George, xi–xii
Washington, Martha, xi
Watercooler® visual, for truth telling,
    123–124, 125–127
The Wealth of Nations (Smith), xix
Welch, Jack, 4
Why We Work (Schwartz), xix, 10,
    95–96
Winning, as goal, 29, 32–33, 35, 37,
    64, 92
Wolfe, David B., 7
Words, alignment of, 48–50, 143
Work
  indifference about, xxi, 18, 19
  meaningful nature of, 18–19, 21,
    25, 95
  money as motivation, xx
Worksheet
  for assessing blind spots, 137–139
  for personal purpose, 26–28
Workshop, xxiii
Wrzesniewski, Amy, 95

Yankelovich, Daniel, 65

About the Authors

JIM HAUDAN is a different kind of leader, with a passion that goes beyond leading Root to success. For more than 25 years, he has been helping organizations unleash hidden potential by fully engaging their people to deliver on the strategies of the business. With his background as a coach, it's not a stretch that the company Jim co-founded focuses on tapping employees' discretionary efforts—the kind that produce winning results.

Root partners with senior teams at major companies worldwide to build creative ways to drive change. A unique blend of 160 business experts, analysts, artists, writers, and educators, the Root team draws an organization's people into the business by appealing to basic human curiosity and intelligence and by combining insights, art, visualization, and dialogue in innovative ways.

Root has worked with more than 850 companies and has impacted millions of people over three decades. Root's story is captured in Jim's bestselling book, *The Art of Engagement: Bridging the Gap Between People and Possibilities* (McGraw-Hill, 2008).

Jim is a frequent speaker on leadership alignment, strategy execution, employee engagement, business transformation, change management, and accelerated learning. He has spoken at TEDx BGSU, Tampa TEDx, and The Conference Board events, and has given the keynote speeches for numerous organizations throughout the world. He has written a weekly column for *Inc.* and contributes to business publications and blogs, such as Switch & Shift, where he was included on the Top 75 List of Human Business Champions.

RICH BERENS has had the opportunity to lead Root and its artists, designers, researchers, programmers, and MBAs in creating breakthrough approaches to change that have reached millions of people around the world for over 10 years.

Rich is a frequent author, thought leader, and speaker on the subject of leadership, transformation, and how to create lasting change. Under Rich's leadership as CEO and Chief Client Fanatic, Root has been listed among the Great Place to Work® Institute's top 25 places to work, been named to the Inc. 5000 fastest-growing companies list, and experienced 10 years of consecutive growth.

Rich joined Root in 1997 after completing his MBA at the University of Michigan.

He worked for Commerzbank in Germany and has lived abroad, in both Germany and Nigeria. He holds a BS in Business Administration from the University of Washington in St. Louis, where he was a three-time All-American tennis player.